FAITH
AND
REASON

ENCYCLICAL LETTER
FIDES ET RATIO
OF THE SUPREME PONTIFF
JOHN PAUL II
ON THE RELATIONSHIP
BETWEEN FAITH AND REASON

MÉDIASPAUL

ISBN 2-89420-164-8

Legal Deposit — 4th Quarter 1998
Bibliothèque nationale du Québec
National Library of Canada

My Venerable Brother Bishops,
Health and the Apostolic Blessing!

F AITH AND REASON are like two wings on which the human spirit rises to the contemplation of truth; and God has placed in the human heart a desire to know the truth—in a word, to know himself—so that, by knowing and loving God, men and women may also come to the fullness of truth about themselves (cf. *Ex* 33:18; *Ps* 27:8-9; 63:2-3; *Jn* 14:8; *1 Jn* 3:2).

INTRODUCTION

"KNOW YOURSELF"

1. In both East and West, we may trace a journey which has led humanity down the centuries to meet and engage truth more and more deeply. It is a journey which has unfolded—as it must—within the horizon of personal self-consciousness: the more human beings know reality and the world, the more they know themselves in their uniqueness, with the question of the meaning of things and of their very existence becoming ever more pressing. This is why all that is

the object of our knowledge becomes a part of our life. The admonition *Know yourself* was carved on the temple portal at Delphi, as testimony to a basic truth to be adopted as a minimal norm by those who seek to set themselves apart from the rest of creation as "human beings", that is as those who "know themselves".

Moreover, a cursory glance at ancient history shows clearly how in different parts of the world, with their different cultures, there arise at the same time the fundamental questions which pervade human life: *Who am I? Where have I come from and where am I going? Why is there evil? What is there after this life?* These are the questions which we find in the sacred writings of Israel, as also in the Veda and the Avesta; we find them in the writings of Confucius and Lao-Tze, and in the preaching of Tirthankara and Buddha; they appear in the poetry of Homer and in the tragedies of Euripides and Sophocles, as they do in the philosophical writings of Plato and Aristotle. They are questions which have their common source in the quest for meaning which has always compelled the human heart. In fact, the answer given to these questions decides the direction which people seek to give to their lives.

2. The Church is no stranger to this journey of discovery, nor could she ever be. From the moment when, through the Paschal Mystery, she received the gift of the ultimate truth about

human life, the Church has made her pilgrim way along the paths of the world to proclaim that Jesus Christ is "the way, and the truth, and the life" (*Jn* 14:6). It is her duty to serve humanity in different ways, but one way in particular imposes a responsibility of a quite special kind: the *diakonia of the truth*.[1] This mission on the one hand makes the believing community a partner in humanity's shared struggle to arrive at truth;[2] and on the other hand it obliges the believing community to proclaim the certitudes arrived at, albeit with a sense that every truth attained is but a step towards that fullness of truth which will appear with the final Revelation of God: "For now we see in a mirror dimly, but then face to face. Now I know in part; then I shall understand fully" (*1 Cor* 13:12).

3.   Men and women have at their disposal an array of resources for generating greater knowledge of truth so that their lives may be ever more human. Among these is *philosophy*, which is directly concerned with asking the question of

[1] In my first Encyclical Letter *Redemptor Hominis*, I wrote: "We have become sharers in this mission of the prophet Christ, and in virtue of that mission we together with him are serving divine truth in the Church. Being responsible for that truth also means loving it and seeking the most exact understanding of it, in order to bring it closer to ourselves and others in all its saving power, its splendour and its profundity joined with simplicity": No. 19: *AAS* 71 (1979), 306.

[2] Cf. SECOND VATICAN ECUMENICAL COUNCIL, Pastoral Constitution on the Church in the Modern World *Gaudium et Spes*, 16.

life's meaning and sketching an answer to it. Philosophy emerges, then, as one of noblest of human tasks. According to its Greek etymology, the term philosophy means "love of wisdom". Born and nurtured when the human being first asked questions about the reason for things and their purpose, philosophy shows in different modes and forms that the desire for truth is part of human nature itself. It is an innate property of human reason to ask why things are as they are, even though the answers which gradually emerge are set within a horizon which reveals how the different human cultures are complementary.

Philosophy's powerful influence on the formation and development of the cultures of the West should not obscure the influence it has also had upon the ways of understanding existence found in the East. Every people has its own native and seminal wisdom which, as a true cultural treasure, tends to find voice and develop in forms which are genuinely philosophical. One example of this is the basic form of philosophical knowledge which is evident to this day in the postulates which inspire national and international legal systems in regulating the life of society.

4.   Nonetheless, it is true that a single term conceals a variety of meanings. Hence the need for a preliminary clarification. Driven by the desire to discover the ultimate truth of existence, human beings seek to acquire those universal elements of knowledge which enable them to under-

stand themselves better and to advance in their own self-realization. These fundamental elements of knowledge spring from the *wonder* awakened in them by the contemplation of creation: human beings are astonished to discover themselves as part of the world, in a relationship with others like them, all sharing a common destiny. Here begins, then, the journey which will lead them to discover ever new frontiers of knowledge. Without wonder, men and women would lapse into deadening routine and little by little would become incapable of a life which is genuinely personal.

Through philosophy's work, the ability to speculate which is proper to the human intellect produces a rigorous mode of thought; and then in turn, through the logical coherence of the affirmations made and the organic unity of their content, it produces a systematic body of knowledge. In different cultural contexts and at different times, this process has yielded results which have produced genuine systems of thought. Yet often enough in history this has brought with it the temptation to identify one single stream with the whole of philosophy. In such cases, we are clearly dealing with a "philosophical pride" which seeks to present its own partial and imperfect view as the complete reading of all reality. In effect, every philosophical *system*, while it should always be respected in its wholeness, without any instrumentalization, must still recognize the primacy of philosophical *enquiry*, from which it stems and which it ought loyally to serve.

Although times change and knowledge increases, it is possible to discern a core of philosophical insight within the history of thought as a whole. Consider, for example, the principles of non-contradiction, finality and causality, as well as the concept of the person as a free and intelligent subject, with the capacity to know God, truth and goodness. Consider as well certain fundamental moral norms which are shared by all. These are among the indications that, beyond different schools of thought, there exists a body of knowledge which may be judged a kind of spiritual heritage of humanity. It is as if we had come upon an *implicit philosophy*, as a result of which all feel that they possess these principles, albeit in a general and unreflective way. Precisely because it is shared in some measure by all, this knowledge should serve as a kind of reference-point for the different philosophical schools. Once reason successfully intuits and formulates the first universal principles of being and correctly draws from them conclusions which are coherent both logically and ethically, then it may be called right reason or, as the ancients called it, *orthōs logos, recta ratio*.

5.   On her part, the Church cannot but set great value upon reason's drive to attain goals which render people's lives ever more worthy. She sees in philosophy the way to come to know

fundamental truths about human life. At the same time, the Church considers philosophy an indispensable help for a deeper understanding of faith and for communicating the truth of the Gospel to those who do not yet know it.

Therefore, following upon similar initiatives by my Predecessors, I wish to reflect upon this special activity of human reason. I judge it necessary to do so because, at the present time in particular, the search for ultimate truth seems often to be neglected. Modern philosophy clearly has the great merit of focusing attention upon man. From this starting-point, human reason with its many questions has developed further its yearning to know more and to know it ever more deeply. Complex systems of thought have thus been built, yielding results in the different fields of knowledge and fostering the development of culture and history. Anthropology, logic, the natural sciences, history, linguistics and so forth—the whole universe of knowledge has been involved in one way or another. Yet the positive results achieved must not obscure the fact that reason, in its one-sided concern to investigate human subjectivity, seems to have forgotten that men and women are always called to direct their steps towards a truth which transcends them. Sundered from that truth, individuals are at the mercy of caprice, and their state as person ends up being judged by pragmatic criteria based essentially upon experimental data, in the mistaken belief that technology must dominate all. It has happened therefore that reason, rather than voicing the human orientation towards truth, has wilted under the weight of so much knowledge and little by little has lost the capacity to lift its gaze to the heights, not daring to rise to the truth of being. Abandoning the investigation of being, modern philosophical research has concentrated instead upon human knowing. Rather than make use of the human capacity to know the truth, modern philosophy has preferred to accentuate the ways in which this capacity is limited and conditioned.

This has given rise to different forms of agnosticism and relativism which have led philosophical research to lose its way in the shifting sands of widespread scepticism. Recent times have seen the rise to prominence of various doctrines which tend to devalue even the truths which had been judged certain. A legitimate plurality of positions has yielded to an undifferentiated pluralism, based upon the assumption that all positions are equally valid, which is one of today's most widespread symptoms of the lack of confidence in truth. Even certain conceptions of life coming from the East betray this lack of confidence, denying truth its exclusive character and assuming that truth reveals itself equally in different doctrines, even if they contradict one another. On this understanding, everything is reduced to opinion; and there is a sense of being adrift. While, on the one hand, philosophical thinking has succeeded in coming closer to the reality of human life and its forms of expression, it has also tended to pursue issues—existential, hermeneutical or linguistic—which ignore the radical question of the truth about personal existence, about being and about God. Hence we see among the men and women of our time, and not just in some philosophers, attitudes of widespread distrust of the human being's great capacity for knowledge. With a false modesty, people rest content with partial and provisional truths, no longer seeking to ask radical questions about the meaning and ultimate foundation of human, personal and social existence. In short, the hope that philosophy might be able to provide definitive answers to these questions has dwindled.

6.   Sure of her competence as the bearer of the Revelation of Jesus Christ, the Church reaffirms the need to reflect upon truth. This is why I have decided to address you, my venerable Brother Bishops, with whom I share the mission of "proclaiming the truth openly" (*2 Cor* 4:2), as also theologians and philosophers whose duty it is to explore the different aspects of truth, and all those who are searching; and I do so in order to offer some reflections on the path which leads to true wisdom, so that those who love truth may take the sure path leading to it and so find rest from their labours and joy for their spirit.

I feel impelled to undertake this task above all because of the Second Vatican Council's insistence that the Bishops are "witnesses of divine and catholic truth".[3] To bear witness to the truth is therefore a task entrusted to us Bishops; we cannot renounce this task without failing in the ministry which we have received. In reaffirming the truth of faith, we can both restore to our contemporaries a genuine trust in their capacity to know and challenge philosophy to recover and develop its own full dignity.

There is a further reason why I write these reflections. In my Encyclical Letter *Veritatis Splendor*, I drew attention to "certain fundamental truths of Catholic doctrine which, in the present circumstances, risk being distorted or denied".[4] In the present Letter, I wish to pursue that reflection by concentrating on the theme of *truth* itself and on its *foundation* in relation to *faith*. For it is undeniable that this time of rapid and complex change can leave especially the younger generation, to whom the future belongs and on whom it depends, with a sense that they have no valid points of reference. The need for a foundation for personal and communal life becomes all the more pressing at a time when we are faced with the patent inadequacy of perspectives in which the ephemeral is affirmed as a value and the possibility of discovering the real meaning of life is cast into doubt. This is why many people stumble through life to the very edge of the

[3] Dogmatic Constitution on the Church *Lumen Gentium*, 25.
[4] No. 4: *AAS* 85 (1993), 1136.

abyss without knowing where they are going. At times, this happens because those whose vocation it is to give cultural expression to their thinking no longer look to truth, preferring quick success to the toil of patient enquiry into what makes life worth living. With its enduring appeal to the search for truth, philosophy has the great responsibility of forming thought and culture; and now it must strive resolutely to recover its original vocation. This is why I have felt both the need and the duty to address this theme so that, on the threshold of the third millennium of the Christian era, humanity may come to a clearer sense of the great resources with which it has been endowed and may commit itself with renewed courage to implement the plan of salvation of which its history is part.

CHAPTER I

THE REVELATION
OF GOD'S WISDOM

Jesus, revealer of the Father

7.   Underlying all the Church's thinking is the awareness that she is the bearer of a message which has its origin in God himself (cf. *2 Cor* 4:1-2). The knowledge which the Church offers to man has its origin not in any speculation of her own, however sublime, but in the word of God which she has received in faith (cf. *1 Th* 2:13). At the origin of our life of faith there is an encounter, unique in kind, which discloses a mystery hidden for long ages (cf. *1 Cor* 2:7; *Rom* 16:25-26) but which is now revealed: "In his goodness and wisdom, God chose to reveal himself and to make known to us the hidden purpose of his will (cf. *Eph* 1:9), by which, through Christ, the Word made flesh, man has access to the Father in the Holy Spirit and comes to share in the divine nature".[5] This initiative is utterly gratuitous, moving from God to men and women in order to bring them to salvation. As the

---

[5] SECOND VATICAN ECUMENICAL COUNCIL, Dogmatic Constitution on Divine Revelation *Dei Verbum*, 2.

source of love, God desires to make himself known; and the knowledge which the human being has of God perfects all that the human mind can know of the meaning of life.

8. Restating almost to the letter the teaching of the First Vatican Council's Constitution *Dei Filius*, and taking into account the principles set out by the Council of Trent, the Second Vatican Council's Constitution *Dei Verbum* pursued the age-old journey of *understanding faith*, reflecting on Revelation in the light of the teaching of Scripture and of the entire Patristic tradition. At the First Vatican Council, the Fathers had stressed the supernatural character of God's Revelation. On the basis of mistaken and very widespread assertions, the rationalist critique of the time attacked faith and denied the possibility of any knowledge which was not the fruit of reason's natural capacities. This obliged the Council to reaffirm emphatically that there exists a knowledge which is peculiar to faith, surpassing the knowledge proper to human reason, which nevertheless by its nature can discover the Creator. This knowledge expresses a truth based upon the very fact of God who reveals himself, a truth which is most certain, since God neither deceives nor wishes to deceive.[6]

9. The First Vatican Council teaches, then, that the truth attained by philosophy and the

[6] Cf. Dogmatic Constitution on the Catholic Faith *Dei Filius*, III: *DS* 3008.

truth of Revelation are neither identical nor mutually exclusive: "There exists a twofold order of knowledge, distinct not only as regards their source, but also as regards their object. With regard to the source, because we know in one by natural reason, in the other by divine faith. With regard to the object, because besides those things which natural reason can attain, there are proposed for our belief mysteries hidden in God which, unless they are divinely revealed, cannot be known".[7] Based upon God's testimony and enjoying the supernatural assistance of grace, faith is of an order other than philosophical knowledge which depends upon sense perception and experience and which advances by the light of the intellect alone. Philosophy and the sciences function within the order of natural reason; while faith, enlightened and guided by the Spirit, recognizes in the message of salvation the "fullness of grace and truth" (cf. *Jn* 1:14) which God has willed to reveal in history and definitively through his Son, Jesus Christ (cf. *1 Jn* 5:9; *Jn* 5:31-32).

10. Contemplating Jesus as revealer, the Fathers of the Second Vatican Council stressed the salvific character of God's Revelation in history, describing it in these terms: "In this Revelation, the invisible God (cf. *Col* 1:15; *1 Tim* 1:17), out of the abundance of his love speaks to men and

---

[7] *Ibid.,* IV: *DS* 3015; quoted also in SECOND VATICAN ECUMENICAL COUNCIL, Pastoral Constitution on the Church in the Modern World *Gaudium et Spes,* 59.

women as friends (cf. *Ex* 33:11; *Jn* 15:14-15) and lives among them (cf. *Bar* 3:38), so that he may invite and take them into communion with himself. This plan of Revelation is realized by deeds and words having an inner unity: the deeds wrought by God in the history of salvation manifest and confirm the teaching and realities signified by the words, while the words proclaim the deeds and clarify the mystery contained in them. By this Revelation, then, the deepest truth about God and human salvation is made clear to us in Christ, who is the mediator and at the same time the fullness of all Revelation".[8]

11.   God's Revelation is therefore immersed in time and history. Jesus Christ took flesh in the "fullness of time" (*Gal* 4:4); and two thousand years later, I feel bound to restate forcefully that "in Christianity time has a fundamental importance".[9] It is within time that the whole work of creation and salvation comes to light; and it emerges clearly above all that, with the Incarnation of the Son of God, our life is even now a foretaste of the fulfilment of time which is to come (cf. *Heb* 1:2).

The truth about himself and his life which God has entrusted to humanity is immersed therefore in time and history; and it was declared once and for all in the mystery of Jesus of

[8] Dogmatic Constitution on Divine Revelation *Dei Verbum*, 2.

[9] Apostolic Letter *Tertio Millennio Adveniente* (10 November 1994), 10: *AAS* 87 (1995), 11.

17

Nazareth. The Constitution *Dei Verbum* puts it eloquently: "After speaking in many places and varied ways through the prophets, God 'last of all in these days has spoken to us by his Son' (*Heb* 1:1-2). For he sent his Son, the eternal Word who enlightens all people, so that he might dwell among them and tell them the innermost realities about God (cf. *Jn* 1:1-18). Jesus Christ, the Word made flesh, sent as 'a human being to human beings', 'speaks the words of God' (*Jn* 3:34), and completes the work of salvation which his Father gave him to do (cf. *Jn* 5:36; 17:4). To see Jesus is to see his Father (*Jn* 14:9). For this reason, Jesus perfected Revelation by fulfilling it through his whole work of making himself present and manifesting himself: through his words and deeds, his signs and wonders, but especially though his death and glorious Resurrection from the dead and finally his sending of the Spirit of truth".[10]

For the People of God, therefore, history becomes a path to be followed to the end, so that by the unceasing action of the Holy Spirit (cf. *Jn* 16:13) the contents of revealed truth may find their full expression. This is the teaching of the Constitution *Dei Verbum* when it states that "as the centuries succeed one another, the Church constantly progresses towards the fullness of di-

[10] No. 4.

vine truth, until the words of God reach their complete fulfilment in her".[11]

12.   History therefore becomes the arena where we see what God does for humanity. God comes to us in the things we know best and can verify most easily, the things of our everyday life, apart from which we cannot understand ourselves.

In the Incarnation of the Son of God we see forged the enduring and definitive synthesis which the human mind of itself could not even have imagined: the Eternal enters time, the Whole lies hidden in the part, God takes on a human face. The truth communicated in Christ's Revelation is therefore no longer confined to a particular place or culture, but is offered to every man and woman who would welcome it as the word which is the absolutely valid source of meaning for human life. Now, in Christ, all have access to the Father, since by his Death and Resurrection Christ has bestowed the divine life which the first Adam had refused (cf. *Rom* 5:12-15). Through this Revelation, men and women are offered the ultimate truth about their own life and about the goal of history. As the Constitution *Gaudium et Spes* puts it, "only in the mystery of the incarnate Word does the mystery of man take on light".[12] Seen in any other terms, the mystery of personal existence remains an insoluble riddle. Where might the human being

[11] No. 8.
[12] No. 22.

19

seek the answer to dramatic questions such as pain, the suffering of the innocent and death, if not in the light streaming from the mystery of Christ's Passion, Death and Resurrection?

Reason before the mystery

13.   It should nonetheless be kept in mind that Revelation remains charged with mystery. It is true that Jesus, with his entire life, revealed the countenance of the Father, for he came to teach the secret things of God.[13] But our vision of the face of God is always fragmentary and impaired by the limits of our understanding. Faith alone makes it possible to penetrate the mystery in a way that allows us to understand it coherently.

The Council teaches that "the obedience of faith must be given to God who reveals himself".[14] This brief but dense statement points to a fundamental truth of Christianity. Faith is said first to be an obedient response to God. This implies that God be acknowledged in his divinity, transcendence and supreme freedom. By the authority of his absolute transcendence, God who makes himself known is also the source of the credibility of what he reveals. By faith, men and women give their *assent* to this divine testimony. This means that they acknowledge fully and integrally the truth of what is revealed because it is

---

[13] Cf. SECOND VATICAN ECUMENICAL COUNCIL, Dogmatic Constitution on Divine Revelation *Dei Verbum*, 4.
    [14] *Ibid.*, 5.

God himself who is the guarantor of that truth. They can make no claim upon this truth which comes to them as gift and which, set within the context of interpersonal communication, urges reason to be open to it and to embrace its profound meaning. This is why the Church has always considered the act of entrusting oneself to God to be a moment of fundamental decision which engages the whole person. In that act, the intellect and the will display their spiritual nature, enabling the subject to act in a way which realizes personal freedom to the full.[15] It is not just that freedom is part of the act of faith: it is absolutely required. Indeed, it is faith that allows individuals to give consummate expression to their own freedom. Put differently, freedom is not realized in decisions made against God. For how could it be an exercise of true freedom to refuse to be open to the very reality which enables our self-realization? Men and women can accomplish no more important act in their lives than the act of faith; it is here that freedom reaches the certainty of truth and chooses to live in that truth.

To assist reason in its effort to understand the mystery there are the signs which Revelation

[15] The First Vatican Council, to which the quotation above refers, teaches that the obedience of faith requires the engagement of the intellect and the will: "Since human beings are totally dependent on God as their creator and Lord, and created reason is completely subject to uncreated truth, we are obliged to yield through faith to God the revealer full submission of intellect and will" (Dogmatic Constitution on the Catholic Faith *Dei Filius*, III: *DS* 3008).

21

itself presents. These serve to lead the search for truth to new depths, enabling the mind in its autonomous exploration to penetrate within the mystery by use of reason's own methods, of which it is rightly jealous. Yet these signs also urge reason to look beyond their status as signs in order to grasp the deeper meaning which they bear. They contain a hidden truth to which the mind is drawn and which it cannot ignore without destroying the very signs which it is given.

In a sense, then, we return to the *sacramental* character of Revelation and especially to the sign of the Eucharist, in which the indissoluble unity between the signifier and signified makes it possible to grasp the depths of the mystery. In the Eucharist, Christ is truly present and alive, working through his Spirit; yet, as Saint Thomas said so well, "what you neither see nor grasp, faith confirms for you, leaving nature far behind; a sign it is that now appears, hiding in mystery realities sublime".[16] He is echoed by the philosopher Pascal: "Just as Jesus Christ went unrecognized among men, so does his truth appear without external difference among common modes of thought. So too does the Eucharist remain among common bread".[17]

In short, the knowledge proper to faith does not destroy the mystery; it only reveals it the more, showing how necessary it is for people's

---

[16] *Sequence* for the Solemnity of the Body and Blood of the Lord.

[17] *Pensées*, 789 (ed. L. Brunschvicg).

lives: Christ the Lord "in revealing the mystery of the Father and his love fully reveals man to himself and makes clear his supreme calling",[18] which is to share in the divine mystery of the life of the Trinity.[19]

14. From the teaching of the two Vatican Councils there also emerges a genuinely novel consideration for philosophical learning. Revelation has set within history a point of reference which cannot be ignored if the mystery of human life is to be known. Yet this knowledge refers back constantly to the mystery of God which the human mind cannot exhaust but can only receive and embrace in faith. Between these two poles, reason has its own specific field in which it can enquire and understand, restricted only by its finiteness before the infinite mystery of God.

Revelation therefore introduces into our history a universal and ultimate truth which stirs the human mind to ceaseless effort; indeed, it impels reason continually to extend the range of its knowledge until it senses that it has done all in its power, leaving no stone unturned. To assist our reflection on this point we have one of the most fruitful and important minds in human history, a point of reference for both philosophy and theology: Saint Anselm. In his *Proslogion*, the

---

[18] SECOND VATICAN ECUMENICAL COUNCIL, Pastoral Constitution on the Church in the Modern World *Gaudium et Spes*, 22.

[19] Cf. SECOND VATICAN ECUMENICAL COUNCIL, Dogmatic Constitution on Divine Revelation *Dei Verbum*, 2.

Archbishop of Canterbury puts it this way: "Thinking of this problem frequently and intently, at times it seemed I was ready to grasp what I was seeking; at other times it eluded my thought completely, until finally, despairing of being able to find it, I wanted to abandon the search for something which was impossible to find. I wanted to rid myself of that thought because, by filling my mind, it distracted me from other problems from which I could gain some profit; but it would then present itself with ever greater insistence... Woe is me, one of the poor children of Eve, far from God, what did I set out to do and what have I accomplished? What was I aiming for and how far have I got? What did I aspire to and what did I long for?... O Lord, you are not only that than which nothing greater can be conceived (*non solum es quo maius cogitari nequit*), but you are greater than all that can be conceived (*quiddam maius quam cogitari possit*)... If you were not such, something greater than you could be thought, but this is impossible".[20]

15. The truth of Christian Revelation, found in Jesus of Nazareth, enables all men and women to embrace the "mystery" of their own life. As absolute truth, it summons human beings to be open to the transcendent, whilst respecting both their autonomy as creatures and their freedom. At this point the relationship between freedom

[20] Proemium and Nos. 1, 15: *PL* 158, 223-224; 226; 235.

and truth is complete, and we understand the full meaning of the Lord's words: "You will know the truth, and the truth will make you free" (*Jn* 8:32).

Christian Revelation is the true lodestar of men and women as they strive to make their way amid the pressures of an immanentist habit of mind and the constrictions of a technocratic logic. It is the ultimate possibility offered by God for the human being to know in all its fullness the seminal plan of love which began with creation. To those wishing to know the truth, if they can look beyond themselves and their own concerns, there is given the possibility of taking full and harmonious possession of their lives, precisely by following the path of truth. Here the words of the Book of Deuteronomy are pertinent: "This commandment which I command you is not too hard for you, neither is it far off. It is not in heaven that you should say, 'Who will go up for us to heaven, and bring it to us, that we may hear it and do it?' Neither is it beyond the sea, that you should say, 'Who will go over the sea for us, and bring it to us, that we may hear and do it?' But the word is very near you; it is in your mouth and in your heart, that you can do it" (30:11-14). This text finds an echo in the famous dictum of the holy philosopher and theologian Augustine: "Do not wander far and wide but return into yourself. Deep within man there dwells the truth" (*Noli foras ire, in te ipsum redi. In interiore homine habitat veritas*).[21]

These considerations prompt a first conclusion: the truth made known to us by Revelation is neither the product nor the consummation of an argument devised by human reason. It appears instead as something gratuitous, which itself stirs thought and seeks acceptance as an expression of love. This revealed truth is set within our history as an anticipation of that ultimate and definitive vision of God which is reserved for those who believe in him and seek him with a sincere heart. The ultimate purpose of personal existence, then, is the theme of philosophy and theology alike. For all their difference of method and content, both disciplines point to that "path of life" (*Ps* 16:11) which, as faith tells us, leads in the end to the full and lasting joy of the contemplation of the Triune God.

---

[21] *De Vera Religione*, XXXIX, 72: *CCL* 32, 234.

CHAPTER II

CREDO UT INTELLEGAM

"Wisdom knows all and understands all" (*Wis* 9:11)

16.   Sacred Scripture indicates with remarkably clear cues how deeply related are the knowledge conferred by faith and the knowledge conferred by reason; and it is in *the Wisdom literature* that this relationship is addressed most explicitly. What is striking about these biblical texts, if they are read without prejudice, is that they embody not only the faith of Israel, but also the treasury of cultures and civilizations which have long vanished. As if by special design, the voices of Egypt and Mesopotamia sound again and certain features common to the cultures of the ancient Near East come to life in these pages which are so singularly rich in deep intuition.

It is no accident that, when the sacred author comes to describe the wise man, he portrays him as one who loves and seeks the truth: "Happy the man who meditates on wisdom and reasons intelligently, who reflects in his heart on her ways and ponders her secrets. He pursues her like a hunter and lies in wait on her paths. He peers through her windows and listens at her doors. He camps near her house and fastens his tent-

27

peg to her walls; he pitches his tent near her and so finds an excellent resting-place; he places his children under her protection and lodges under her boughs; by her he is sheltered from the heat and he dwells in the shade of her glory" (*Sir* 14:20-27).

For the inspired writer, as we see, the desire for knowledge is characteristic of all people. Intelligence enables everyone, believer and non-believer, to reach "the deep waters" of knowledge (cf. *Prov* 20:5). It is true that ancient Israel did not come to knowledge of the world and its phenomena by way of abstraction, as did the Greek philosopher or the Egyptian sage. Still less did the good Israelite understand knowledge in the way of the modern world which tends more to distinguish different kinds of knowing. Nonetheless, the biblical world has made its own distinctive contribution to the theory of knowledge.

What is distinctive in the biblical text is the conviction that there is a profound and indissoluble unity between the knowledge of reason and the knowledge of faith. The world and all that happens within it, including history and the fate of peoples, are realities to be observed, analysed and assessed with all the resources of reason, but without faith ever being foreign to the process. Faith intervenes not to abolish reason's autonomy nor to reduce its scope for action, but solely to bring the human being to understand that in these events it is the God of Israel who acts. Thus the world and the events of history cannot be understood in depth without professing faith in the God who is at work in them. Faith sharpens the inner eye, opening the mind to discover in the flux of events the workings of Providence. Here the words of the Book of Proverbs are pertinent: "The human mind plans the way, but the Lord directs the steps" (16:9). This is to say that with the light of reason human beings can know which path to take, but they can follow that path to its end, quickly and unhindered, only if with a rightly tuned spirit they search for it within the horizon of faith. Therefore, reason and faith cannot be separated without diminishing the capacity of men and women to know themselves, the world and God in an appropriate way.

17. There is thus no reason for competition of any kind between reason and faith: each contains the other, and each has its own scope for action. Again the Book of Proverbs points in this direction when it exclaims: "It is the glory of God to conceal things, but the glory of kings is to search things out" (*Prov* 25:2). In their respective worlds, God and the human being are set within a unique relationship. In God there lies the origin of all things, in him is found the fullness of the mystery, and in this his glory consists; to men and women there falls the task of exploring truth with their reason, and in this their nobility consists. The Psalmist adds one final piece to this mosaic when he says in prayer: "How deep to me are your thoughts, O God! How vast is the

sum of them! If I try to count them, they are more than the sand. If I come to the end, I am still with you" (139:17-18). The desire for knowledge is so great and it works in such a way that the human heart, despite its experience of insurmountable limitation, yearns for the infinite riches which lie beyond, knowing that there is to be found the satisfying answer to every question as yet unanswered.

18.   We may say, then, that Israel, with her reflection, was able to open to reason the path that leads to the mystery. With the Revelation of God Israel could plumb the depths of all that she sought in vain to reach by way of reason. On the basis of this deeper form of knowledge, the Chosen People understood that, if reason were to be fully true to itself, then it must respect certain basic rules. The first of these is that reason must realize that human knowledge is a journey which allows no rest; the second stems from the awareness that such a path is not for the proud who think that everything is the fruit of personal conquest; a third rule is grounded in the "fear of God" whose transcendent sovereignty and provident love in the governance of the world reason must recognize.

In abandoning these rules, the human being runs the risk of failure and ends up in the condition of "the fool". For the Bible, in this foolishness there lies a threat to life. The fool thinks that he knows many things, but really he is incapable of fixing his gaze on the things that truly matter. Therefore he can neither order his mind (*Prov* 1:7) nor assume a correct attitude to himself or to the world around him. And so when he claims that "God does not exist" (cf. *Ps* 14:1), he shows with absolute clarity just how deficient his knowledge is and just how far he is from the full truth of things, their origin and their destiny.

19. The Book of Wisdom contains several important texts which cast further light on this theme. There the sacred author speaks of God who reveals himself in nature. For the ancients, the study of the natural sciences coincided in large part with philosophical learning. Having affirmed that with their intelligence human beings can "know the structure of the world and the activity of the elements... the cycles of the year and the constellations of the stars, the natures of animals and the tempers of wild beasts" (*Wis* 7:17, 19-20)—in a word, that he can philosophize—the sacred text takes a significant step forward. Making his own the thought of Greek philosophy, to which he seems to refer in the context, the author affirms that, in reasoning about nature, the human being can rise to God: "From the greatness and beauty of created things comes a corresponding perception of their Creator" (*Wis* 13:5). This is to recognize as a first stage of divine Revelation the marvellous "book of nature", which, when read with the proper tools of

human reason, can lead to knowledge of the Creator. If human beings with their intelligence fail to recognize God as Creator of all, it is not because they lack the means to do so, but because their free will and their sinfulness place an impediment in the way.

20.   Seen in this light, reason is valued without being overvalued. The results of reasoning may in fact be true, but these results acquire their true meaning only if they are set within the larger horizon of faith: "All man's steps are ordered by the Lord: how then can man understand his own ways?" (*Prov* 20:24). For the Old Testament, then, faith liberates reason in so far as it allows reason to attain correctly what it seeks to know and to place it within the ultimate order of things, in which everything acquires true meaning. In brief, human beings attain truth by way of reason because, enlightened by faith, they discover the deeper meaning of all things and most especially of their own existence. Rightly, therefore, the sacred author identifies the fear of God as the beginning of true knowledge: "The fear of the Lord is the beginning of knowledge" (*Prov* 1:7; cf. *Sir* 1:14).

"Acquire wisdom, acquire understanding" (Prov 4:5)

21.   For the Old Testament, knowledge is not simply a matter of careful observation of the

human being, of the world and of history, but supposes as well an indispensable link with faith and with what has been revealed. These are the challenges which the Chosen People had to confront and to which they had to respond. Pondering this as his situation, biblical man discovered that he could understand himself only as "being in relation"—with himself, with people, with the world and with God. This opening to the mystery, which came to him through Revelation, was for him, in the end, the source of true knowledge. It was this which allowed his reason to enter the realm of the infinite where an understanding for which until then he had not dared to hope became a possibility.

For the sacred author, the task of searching for the truth was not without the strain which comes once the limits of reason are reached. This is what we find, for example, when the Book of Proverbs notes the weariness which comes from the effort to understand the mysterious designs of God (cf. 30:1-6). Yet, for all the toil involved, believers do not surrender. They can continue on their way to the truth because they are certain that God has created them "explorers" (cf. *Qoh* 1:13), whose mission it is to leave no stone unturned, though the temptation to doubt is always there. Leaning on God, they continue to reach out, always and everywhere, for all that is beautiful, good and true.

22.   In the first chapter of his Letter to the Romans, Saint Paul helps us to appreciate better

the depth of insight of the Wisdom literature's reflection. Developing a philosophical argument in popular language, the Apostle declares a profound truth: through all that is created the "eyes of the mind" can come to know God. Through the medium of creatures, God stirs in reason an intuition of his "power" and his "divinity" (cf. *Rom* 1:20). This is to concede to human reason a capacity which seems almost to surpass its natural limitations. Not only is it not restricted to sensory knowledge, from the moment that it can reflect critically upon the data of the senses, but, by discoursing on the data provided by the senses, reason can reach the cause which lies at the origin of all perceptible reality. In philosophical terms, we could say that this important Pauline text affirms the human capacity for metaphysical enquiry.

According to the Apostle, it was part of the original plan of the creation that reason should without difficulty reach beyond the sensory data to the origin of all things: the Creator. But because of the disobedience by which man and woman chose to set themselves in full and absolute autonomy in relation to the One who had created them, this ready access to God the Creator diminished.

This is the human condition vividly described by the Book of Genesis when it tells us that God placed the human being in the Garden of Eden, in the middle of which there stood "the tree of knowledge of good and evil" (2:17). The symbol is clear: man was in no position to discern and decide for himself what was good and what was evil, but was constrained to appeal to a higher source. The blindness of pride deceived our first parents into thinking themselves sovereign and autonomous, and into thinking that they could ignore the knowledge which comes from God. All men and women were caught up in this primal disobedience, which so wounded reason that from then on its path to full truth would be strewn with obstacles. From that time onwards the human capacity to know the truth was impaired by an aversion to the One who is the source and origin of truth. It is again the Apostle who reveals just how far human thinking, because of sin, became "empty", and human reasoning became distorted and inclined to falsehood (cf. *Rom* 1:21-22). The eyes of the mind were no longer able to see clearly: reason became more and more a prisoner to itself. The coming of Christ was the saving event which redeemed reason from its weakness, setting it free from the shackles in which it had imprisoned itself.

23.   This is why the Christian's relationship to philosophy requires thorough-going discernment. In the New Testament, especially in the Letters of Saint Paul, one thing emerges with great clarity: the opposition between "the wisdom of this world" and the wisdom of God revealed in Jesus

Christ. The depth of revealed wisdom disrupts the cycle of our habitual patterns of thought, which are in no way able to express that wisdom in its fullness.

The beginning of the First Letter to the Corinthians poses the dilemma in a radical way. The crucified Son of God is the historic event upon which every attempt of the mind to construct an adequate explanation of the meaning of existence upon merely human argumentation comes to grief. The true key-point, which challenges every philosophy, is Jesus Christ's death on the Cross. It is here that every attempt to reduce the Father's saving plan to purely human logic is doomed to failure. "Where is the one who is wise? Where is the learned? Where is the debater of this age? Has not God made foolish the wisdom of the world?" (*1 Cor* 1:20), the Apostle asks emphatically. The wisdom of the wise is no longer enough for what God wants to accomplish; what is required is a decisive step towards welcoming something radically new: "God chose what is foolish in the world to shame the wise...; God chose what is low and despised in the world, things that are not to reduce to nothing things that are" (*1 Cor* 1:27-28). Human wisdom refuses to see in its own weakness the possibility of its strength; yet Saint Paul is quick to affirm: "When I am weak, then I am strong" (*2 Cor* 12:10). Man cannot grasp how death could be the source of life and love; yet to reveal the mystery of his saving plan God has chosen precisely that which reason considers "foolishness" and a "scandal". Adopting the language of the philosophers of his time, Paul comes to the summit of his teaching as he speaks the paradox: "God has chosen in the world... that which is nothing to reduce to nothing things that are" (cf. *1 Cor* 1:28). In order to express the gratuitous nature of the love revealed in the Cross of Christ, the Apostle is not afraid to use the most radical language of the philosophers in their thinking about God. Reason cannot eliminate the mystery of love which the Cross represents, while the Cross can give to reason the ultimate answer which it seeks. It is not the wisdom of words, but the Word of Wisdom which Saint Paul offers as the criterion of both truth and salvation.

The wisdom of the Cross, therefore, breaks free of all cultural limitations which seek to contain it and insists upon an openness to the universality of the truth which it bears. What a challenge this is to our reason, and how great the gain for reason if it yields to this wisdom! Of itself, philosophy is able to recognize the human being's ceaselessly self-transcendent orientation towards the truth; and, with the assistance of faith, it is capable of accepting the "foolishness" of the Cross as the authentic critique of those who delude themselves that they possess the truth, when in fact they run it aground on the shoals of a system of their own devising. The preaching of

Christ crucified and risen is the reef upon which the link between faith and philosophy can break up, but it is also the reef beyond which the two can set forth upon the boundless ocean of truth. Here we see not only the border between reason and faith, but also the space where the two may meet.

CHAPTER III

INTELLEGO UT CREDAM

Journeying in search of truth

24.   In the Acts of the Apostles, the Evangelist Luke tells of Paul's coming to Athens on one of his missionary journeys. The city of philosophers was full of statues of various idols. One altar in particular caught his eye, and he took this as a convenient starting-point to establish a common base for the proclamation of the kerygma. "Athenians," he said, "I see how extremely religious you are in every way. For as I went through the city and looked carefully at the objects of your worship, I found among them an altar with the inscription, 'To an unknown god'. What therefore you worship as unknown, this I proclaim to you" (*Acts* 17:22-23). From this starting-point, Saint Paul speaks of God as Creator, as the One who transcends all things and gives life to all. He then continues his speech in these terms: "From one ancestor he made all nations to inhabit the whole earth, and he allotted the times of their existence and the boundaries of the places where they would live, so that they would search for God and perhaps grope for him and find

39

him—though indeed he is not far from each one of us" (*Acts* 17:26-27).

The Apostle accentuates a truth which the Church has always treasured: in the far reaches of the human heart there is a seed of desire and nostalgia for God. The Liturgy of Good Friday recalls this powerfully when, in praying for those who do not believe, we say: "Almighty and eternal God, you created mankind so that all might long to find you and have peace when you are found".[22] There is therefore a path which the human being may choose to take, a path which begins with reason's capacity to rise beyond what is contingent and set out towards the infinite.

In different ways and at different times, men and women have shown that they can articulate this intimate desire of theirs. Through literature, music, painting, sculpture, architecture and every other work of their creative intelligence they have declared the urgency of their quest. In a special way philosophy has made this search its own and, with its specific tools and scholarly methods, has articulated this universal human desire.

25.   "All human beings desire to know",[23] and truth is the proper object of this desire. Everyday life shows how concerned each of us is to discover for ourselves, beyond mere opinions, how things really are. Within visible creation, man is

---

[22] "*Ut te semper desiderando quaererent et inveniendo quiescerent*": *Missale Romanum.*

[23] ARISTOTLE, *Metaphysics,* I, 1.

the only creature who not only is capable of knowing but who knows that he knows, and is therefore interested in the real truth of what he perceives. People cannot be genuinely indifferent to the question of whether what they know is true or not. If they discover that it is false, they reject it; but if they can establish its truth, they feel themselves rewarded. It is this that Saint Augustine teaches when he writes: "I have met many who wanted to deceive, but none who wanted to be deceived".[24] It is rightly claimed that persons have reached adulthood when they can distinguish independently between truth and falsehood, making up their own minds about the objective reality of things. This is what has driven so many enquiries, especially in the scientific field, which in recent centuries have produced important results, leading to genuine progress for all humanity.

No less important than research in the theoretical field is research in the practical field—by which I mean the search for truth which looks to the good which is to be performed. In acting ethically, according to a free and rightly tuned will, the human person sets foot upon the path to happiness and moves towards perfection. Here too it is a question of truth. It is this conviction which I stressed in my Encyclical Letter *Veritatis Splendor:* "There is no morality without freedom... Although each individual has a right to be

[24] *Confessions,* X, 23, 33: CCL 27, 173.

41

respected in his own journey in search of the truth, there exists a prior moral obligation, and a grave one at that, to seek the truth and to adhere to it once it is known".[25]

It is essential, therefore, that the values chosen and pursued in one's life be true, because only true values can lead people to realize themselves fully, allowing them to be true to their nature. The truth of these values is to be found not by turning in on oneself but by opening oneself to apprehend that truth even at levels which transcend the person. This is an essential condition for us to become ourselves and to grow as mature, adult persons.

26.   The truth comes initially to the human being as a question: *Does life have a meaning? Where is it going?* At first sight, personal existence may seem completely meaningless. It is not necessary to turn to the philosophers of the absurd or to the provocative questioning found in the Book of Job in order to have doubts about life's meaning. The daily experience of suffering—in one's own life and in the lives of others—and the array of facts which seem inexplicable to reason are enough to ensure that a question as dramatic as the question of meaning cannot be evaded.[26] Moreover, the first absolutely certain truth of our life, beyond the fact that we

[25] No. 34: *AAS* 85 (1993), 1161.

[26] Cf. JOHN PAUL II, Apostolic Letter *Salvifici Doloris* (11 February 1984), 9: *AAS* 76 (1984), 209-210.

exist, is the inevitability of our death. Given this unsettling fact, the search for a full answer is inescapable. Each of us has both the desire and the duty to know the truth of our own destiny. We want to know if death will be the definitive end of our life or if there is something beyond—if it is possible to hope for an after-life or not. It is not insignificant that the death of Socrates gave philosophy one of its decisive orientations, no less decisive now than it was more than two thousand years ago. It is not by chance, then, that faced with the fact of death philosophers have again and again posed this question, together with the question of the meaning of life and immortality.

27.   No-one can avoid this questioning, neither the philosopher nor the ordinary person. The answer we give will determine whether or not we think it possible to attain universal and absolute truth; and this is a decisive moment of the search. Every truth—if it really is truth—presents itself as universal, even if it is not the whole truth. If something is true, then it must be true for all people and at all times. Beyond this universality, however, people seek an absolute which might give to all their searching a meaning and an answer—something ultimate, which might serve as the ground of all things. In other words, they seek a final explanation, a supreme value, which refers to nothing beyond itself and which puts an end to all questioning. Hypotheses may

fascinate, but they do not satisfy. Whether we admit it or not, there comes for everyone the moment when personal existence must be anchored to a truth recognized as final, a truth which confers a certitude no longer open to doubt.

Through the centuries, philosophers have sought to discover and articulate such a truth, giving rise to various systems and schools of thought. But beyond philosophical systems, people seek in different ways to shape a "philosophy" of their own—in personal convictions and experiences, in traditions of family and culture, or in journeys in search of life's meaning under the guidance of a master. What inspires all of these is the desire to reach the certitude of truth and the certitude of its absolute value.

The different faces of human truth

28.   The search for truth, of course, is not always so transparent nor does it always produce such results. The natural limitation of reason and the inconstancy of the heart often obscure and distort a person's search. Truth can also drown in a welter of other concerns. People can even run from the truth as soon as they glimpse it because they are afraid of its demands. Yet, for all that they may evade it, the truth still influences life. Life in fact can never be grounded upon doubt, uncertainty or deceit; such an existence would be threatened constantly by fear and anxi-

ety. One may define the human being, therefore, as *the one who seeks the truth*.

29.   It is unthinkable that a search so deeply rooted in human nature would be completely vain and useless. The capacity to search for truth and to pose questions itself implies the rudiments of a response. Human beings would not even begin to search for something of which they knew nothing or for something which they thought was wholly beyond them. Only the sense that they can arrive at an answer leads them to take the first step. This is what normally happens in scientific research. When scientists, following their intuition, set out in search of the logical and verifiable explanation of a phenomenon, they are confident from the first that they will find an answer, and they do not give up in the face of setbacks. They do not judge their original intuition useless simply because they have not reached their goal; rightly enough they will say that they have not yet found a satisfactory answer.

The same must be equally true of the search for truth when it comes to the ultimate questions. The thirst for truth is so rooted in the human heart that to be obliged to ignore it would cast our existence into jeopardy. Everyday life shows well enough how each one of us is preoccupied by the pressure of a few fundamental questions and how in the soul of each of us there is at least an outline of the answers. One reason why the truth of these answers convinces is that they are no different in substance from the answers to which many others have come. To be sure, not every truth to which we come has the same value. But the sum of the results achieved confirms that in principle the human being can arrive at the truth.

30.   It may help, then, to turn briefly to the different modes of truth. Most of them depend upon immediate evidence or are confirmed by experimentation. This is the mode of truth proper to everyday life and to scientific research. At another level we find philosophical truth, attained by means of the speculative powers of the human intellect. Finally, there are religious truths which are to some degree grounded in philosophy, and which we find in the answers which the different religious traditions offer to the ultimate questions.[27]

The truths of philosophy, it should be said, are not restricted only to the sometimes ephemeral teachings of professional philosophers. All men and women, as I have noted, are in some sense philosophers and have their own philosophical conceptions with which they direct their lives. In one way or other, they shape a comprehensive vision and an answer to the question of life's meaning; and in the light of this they interpret their own life's course and regulate their behaviour. At this point, we may pose the question

[27] Cf. SECOND VATICAN ECUMENICAL COUNCIL, Declaration on the Relations of the Church with Non-Christian Religions, *Nostra Aetate,* 2.

of the link between, on the one hand, the truths of philosophy and religion and, on the other, the truth revealed in Jesus Christ. But before tackling that question, one last datum of philosophy needs to be weighed.

31.   Human beings are not made to live alone. They are born into a family and in a family they grow, eventually entering society through their activity. From birth, therefore, they are immersed in traditions which give them not only a language and a cultural formation but also a range of truths in which they believe almost instinctively. Yet personal growth and maturity imply that these same truths can be cast into doubt and evaluated through a process of critical enquiry. It may be that, after this time of transition, these truths are "recovered" as a result of the experience of life or by dint of further reasoning. Nonetheless, there are in the life of a human being many more truths which are simply believed than truths which are acquired by way of personal verification. Who, for instance, could assess critically the countless scientific findings upon which modern life is based? Who could personally examine the flow of information which comes day after day from all parts of the world and which is generally accepted as true? Who in the end could forge anew the paths of experience and thought which have yielded the treasures of human wisdom and religion? This means that the human being—the one who seeks the truth—is also *the one who lives by belief.*

32.   In believing, we entrust ourselves to the knowledge acquired by other people. This suggests an important tension. On the one hand, the knowledge acquired through belief can seem an imperfect form of knowledge, to be perfected gradually through personal accumulation of evidence; on the other hand, belief is often humanly richer than mere evidence, because it involves an interpersonal relationship and brings into play not only a person's capacity to know but also the deeper capacity to entrust oneself to others, to enter into a relationship with them which is intimate and enduring.

It should be stressed that the truths sought in this interpersonal relationship are not primarily empirical or philosophical. Rather, what is sought is *the truth of the person*—what the person is and what the person reveals from deep within. Human perfection, then, consists not simply in acquiring an abstract knowledge of the truth, but in a dynamic relationship of faithful self-giving with others. It is in this faithful self-giving that a person finds a fullness of certainty and security. At the same time, however, knowledge through belief, grounded as it is on trust between persons, is linked to truth: in the act of believing, men and women entrust themselves to the truth which the other declares to them.

Any number of examples could be found to demonstrate this; but I think immediately of the martyrs, who are the most authentic witnesses to the truth about existence. The martyrs know that

they have found the truth about life in the encounter with Jesus Christ, and nothing and no-
one could ever take this certainty from them.
Neither suffering nor violent death could ever
lead them to abandon the truth which they have
discovered in the encounter with Christ. This is
why to this day the witness of the martyrs continues to arouse such interest, to draw agreement,
to win such a hearing and to invite emulation.
This is why their word inspires such confidence:
from the moment they speak to us of what we
perceive deep down as the truth we have sought
for so long, the martyrs provide evidence of a
love that has no need of lengthy arguments in order to convince. The martyrs stir in us a profound trust because they give voice to what we
already feel and they declare what we would like
to have the strength to express.

33.   Step by step, then, we are assembling the
terms of the question. It is the nature of the human being to seek the truth. This search looks
not only to the attainment of truths which are
partial, empirical or scientific; nor is it only in individual acts of decision-making that people seek
the true good. Their search looks towards an ul-
terior truth which would explain the meaning of
life. And it is therefore a search which can reach
its end only in reaching the absolute.[28] Thanks to

[28] This is a theme which I have long pursued and which I
have addressed on a number of occasions. " 'What is man and
of what use is he? What is good in him and what is evil?' (*Sir*

the inherent capacities of thought, man is able to encounter and recognize a truth of this kind. Such a truth—vital and necessary as it is for life—is attained not only by way of reason but also through trusting acquiescence to other persons who can guarantee the authenticity and certainty of the truth itself. There is no doubt that the capacity to entrust oneself and one's life to another person and the decision to do so are among the most significant and expressive human acts.

It must not be forgotten that reason too needs to be sustained in all its searching by trusting dialogue and sincere friendship. A climate of suspicion and distrust, which can beset speculative research, ignores the teaching of the ancient

18:8)... These are questions in every human heart, as the poetic genius of every time and every people has shown, posing again and again—almost as the prophetic voice of humanity—the *serious question* which makes human beings truly what they are. They are questions which express the urgency of finding a reason for existence, in every moment, at life's most important and decisive times as well as more ordinary times. These questions show the deep reasonableness of human existence, since they summon human intelligence and will to search freely for a solution which can reveal the full meaning of life. These enquiries, therefore, are the highest expression of human nature; which is why the answer to them is the gauge of the depth of his engagement with his own existence. In particular, when *the why of things* is explored in full harmony with the search for the ultimate answer, then human reason reaches its zenith and opens to the religious impulse. The religious impulse is the highest expression of the human person, because it is the highpoint of his rational nature. It springs from the profound human aspiration for the truth and it is the basis of the human being's free and personal search for the divine": General Audience (19 October 1983), 1-2: *Insegnamenti* VI, 2 (1983), 814-815.

philosophers who proposed friendship as one of the most appropriate contexts for sound philosophical enquiry.

From all that I have said to this point it emerges that men and women are on a journey of discovery which is humanly unstoppable—a search for the truth and a search for a person to whom they might entrust themselves. Christian faith comes to meet them, offering the concrete possibility of reaching the goal which they seek. Moving beyond the stage of simple believing, Christian faith immerses human beings in the order of grace, which enables them to share in the mystery of Christ, which in turn offers them a true and coherent knowledge of the Triune God. In Jesus Christ, who is the Truth, faith recognizes the ultimate appeal to humanity, an appeal made in order that what we experience as desire and nostalgia may come to its fulfilment.

34.   This truth, which God reveals to us in Jesus Christ, is not opposed to the truths which philosophy perceives. On the contrary, the two modes of knowledge lead to truth in all its fullness. The unity of truth is a fundamental premise of human reasoning, as the principle of non-contradiction makes clear. Revelation renders this unity certain, showing that the God of creation is also the God of salvation history. It is the one and the same God who establishes and guarantees the intelligibility and reasonableness of the natural order of things upon which scientists con-

fidently depend,[29] and who reveals himself as the Father of our Lord Jesus Christ. This unity of truth, natural and revealed, is embodied in a living and personal way in Christ, as the Apostle reminds us: "Truth is in Jesus" (cf. *Eph* 4:21; *Col* 1:15-20). He is the *eternal Word* in whom all things were created, and he is the *incarnate Word* who in his entire person [30] reveals the Father (cf. *Jn* 1:14, 18). What human reason seeks "without knowing it" (cf. *Acts* 17:23) can be found only through Christ: what is revealed in him is "the full truth" (cf. *Jn* 1:14-16) of everything which was created in him and through him and which therefore in him finds its fulfilment (cf. *Col* 1:17).

35. On the basis of these broad considerations, we must now explore more directly the relationship between revealed truth and philosophy. This relationship imposes a twofold consideration,

---

[29] "[Galileo] declared explicitly that the two truths, of faith and of science, can never contradict each other, 'Sacred Scripture and the natural world proceeding equally from the divine Word, the first as dictated by the Holy Spirit, the second as a very faithful executor of the commands of God', as he wrote in his letter to Father Benedetto Castelli on 21 December 1613. The Second Vatican Council says the same thing, even adopting similar language in its teaching: 'Methodical research, in all realms of knowledge, if it respects... moral norms, will never be genuinely opposed to faith: the reality of the world and of faith have their origin in the same God' (*Gaudium et Spes,* 36). Galileo sensed in his scientific research the presence of the Creator who, stirring in the depths of his spirit, stimulated him, anticipating and assisting his intuitions": JOHN PAUL II, Address to the Pontifical Academy of Sciences (10 November 1979): *Insegnamenti,* II, 2 (1979), 1111-1112.

[30] Cf. SECOND VATICAN ECUMENICAL COUNCIL, Dogmatic Constitution on Divine Revelation, *Dei Verbum,* 4.

since the truth conferred by Revelation is a truth to be understood in the light of reason. It is this duality alone which allows us to specify correctly the relationship between revealed truth and philosophical learning. First, then, let us consider the links between faith and philosophy in the course of history. From this, certain principles will emerge as useful reference-points in the attempt to establish the correct link between the two orders of knowledge.

CHAPTER IV

THE RELATIONSHIP
BETWEEN FAITH AND REASON

*Important moments in the encounter of faith
and reason*

36.　The Acts of the Apostles provides evidence that Christian proclamation was engaged from the very first with the philosophical currents of the time. In Athens, we read, Saint Paul entered into discussion with "certain Epicurean and Stoic philosophers" (17:18); and exegetical analysis of his speech at the Areopagus has revealed frequent allusions to popular beliefs deriving for the most part from Stoicism. This is by no means accidental. If pagans were to understand them, the first Christians could not refer only to "Moses and the prophets" when they spoke. They had to point as well to natural knowledge of God and to the voice of conscience.in every human being (cf. *Rom* 1:19-21; 2:14-15; *Acts* 14:16-17). Since in pagan religion this natural knowledge had lapsed into idolatry (cf. *Rom* 1:21-32), the Apostle judged it wiser in his speech to make the link with the thinking of the philosophers, who had always set in opposition to the myths and mystery cults notions more respectful of divine transcendence.

One of the major concerns of classical philosophy was to purify human notions of God of mythological elements. We know that Greek religion, like most cosmic religions, was polytheistic, even to the point of divinizing natural things and phenomena. Human attempts to understand the origin of the gods and hence the origin of the universe find their earliest expression in poetry; and the theogonies remain the first evidence of this human search. But it was the task of the fathers of philosophy to bring to light the link between reason and religion. As they broadened their view to include universal principles, they no longer rested content with the ancient myths, but wanted to provide a rational foundation for their belief in the divinity. This opened a path which took its rise from ancient traditions but allowed a development satisfying the demands of universal reason. This development sought to acquire a critical awareness of what they believed in, and the concept of divinity was the prime beneficiary of this. Superstitions were recognized for what they were and religion was, at least in part, purified by rational analysis. It was on this basis that the Fathers of the Church entered into fruitful dialogue with ancient philosophy, which offered new ways of proclaiming and understanding the God of Jesus Christ.

37.   In tracing Christianity's adoption of philosophy, one should not forget how cautiously

Christians regarded other elements of the cultural world of paganism, one example of which is gnosticism. It was easy to confuse philosophy—understood as practical wisdom and an education for life—with a higher and esoteric kind of knowledge, reserved to those few who were perfect. It is surely this kind of esoteric speculation which Saint Paul has in mind when he puts the Colossians on their guard: "See to it that no-one takes you captive through philosophy and empty deceit, according to human tradition, according to the elemental spirits of the universe and not according to Christ" (2:8). The Apostle's words seem all too pertinent now if we apply them to the various kinds of esoteric superstition widespread today, even among some believers who lack a proper critical sense. Following Saint Paul, other writers of the early centuries, especially Saint Irenaeus and Tertullian, sound the alarm when confronted with a cultural perspective which sought to subordinate the truth of Revelation to the interpretation of the philosophers.

38.   Christianity's engagement with philosophy was therefore neither straight-forward nor immediate. The practice of philosophy and attendance at philosophical schools seemed to the first Christians more of a disturbance than an opportunity. For them, the first and most urgent task was the proclamation of the Risen Christ by way of a personal encounter which would bring the listener to conversion of heart and the request for

Baptism. But that does not mean that they ignored the task of deepening the understanding of faith and its motivations. Quite the contrary. That is why the criticism of Celsus—that Christians were "illiterate and uncouth"[31]—is unfounded and untrue. Their initial disinterest is to be explained on other grounds. The encounter with the Gospel offered such a satisfying answer to the hitherto unresolved question of life's meaning that delving into the philosophers seemed to them something remote and in some ways outmoded.

That seems still more evident today, if we think of Christianity's contribution to the affirmation of the right of everyone to have access to the truth. In dismantling barriers of race, social status and gender, Christianity proclaimed from the first the equality of all men and women before God. One prime implication of this touched the theme of truth. The elitism which had characterized the ancients' search for truth was clearly abandoned. Since access to the truth enables access to God, it must be denied to none. There are many paths which lead to truth, but since Christian truth has a salvific value, any one of these paths may be taken, as long as it leads to the final goal, that is to the Revelation of Jesus Christ.

A pioneer of positive engagement with philosophical thinking—albeit with cautious discern-

---

[31] ORIGEN, *Contra Celsum,* 3, 55: *SC* 136, 130.

ment—was Saint Justin. Although he continued to hold Greek philosophy in high esteem after his conversion, Justin claimed with power and clarity that he had found in Christianity "the only sure and profitable philosophy".[32] Similarly, Clement of Alexandria called the Gospel "the true philosophy",[33] and he understood philosophy, like the Mosaic Law, as instruction which prepared for Christian faith[34] and paved the way for the Gospel.[35] Since "philosophy yearns for the wisdom which consists in rightness of soul and speech and in purity of life, it is well disposed towards wisdom and does all it can to acquire it. We call philosophers those who love the wisdom that is creator and mistress of all things, that is knowledge of the Son of God".[36] For Clement, Greek philosophy is not meant in the first place to bolster and complete Christian truth. Its task is rather the defence of the faith: "The teaching of the Saviour is perfect in itself and has no need of support, because it is the strength and the wisdom of God. Greek philosophy, with its contribution, does not strengthen truth; but, in rendering the attack of sophistry impotent and in disarming those who betray truth and wage war upon it, Greek philosophy is rightly called the

[32] *Dialogue with Trypho,* 8, 1: *PG* 6, 492.
[33] *Stromata* I, 18, 90, 1: *SC* 30, 115.
[34] Cf. *ibid.,* I, 16, 80, 5: *SC* 30, 108.
[35] Cf. *ibid.*, I, 5, 28, 1: *SC* 30, 65.
[36] *Ibid.,* VI, 7, 55, 1-2: *PG* 9, 277.

hedge and the protective wall around the vineyard".[37]

39.   It is clear from history, then, that Christian thinkers were critical in adopting philosophical thought. Among the early examples of this, Origen is certainly outstanding. In countering the attacks launched by the philosopher Celsus, Origen adopts Platonic philosophy to shape his argument and mount his reply. Assuming many elements of Platonic thought, he begins to construct an early form of Christian theology. The name "theology" itself, together with the idea of theology as rational discourse about God, had to this point been tied to its Greek origins. In Aristotelian philosophy, for example, the name signified the noblest part and the true summit of philosophical discourse. But in the light of Christian Revelation what had signified a generic doctrine about the gods assumed a wholly new meaning, signifying now the reflection undertaken by the believer in order to express *the true doctrine* about God. As it developed, this new Christian thought made use of philosophy, but at the same time tended to distinguish itself clearly from philosophy. History shows how Platonic thought, once adopted by theology, underwent profound changes, especially with regard to concepts such as the immortality of the soul, the divinization of man and the origin of evil.

[37] *Ibid.*, I, 20, 100, 1: *SC* 30, 124.

40. In this work of christianizing Platonic and Neo-Platonic thought, the Cappadocian Fathers, Dionysius called the Areopagite and especially Saint Augustine were important. The great Doctor of the West had come into contact with different philosophical schools, but all of them left him disappointed. It was when he encountered the truth of Christian faith that he found strength to undergo the radical conversion to which the philosophers he had known had been powerless to lead him. He himself reveals his motive: "From this time on, I gave my preference to the Catholic faith. I thought it more modest and not in the least misleading to be told by the Church to believe what could not be demonstrated—whether that was because a demonstration existed but could not be understood by all or whether the matter was not one open to rational proof—rather than from the Manichees to have a rash promise of knowledge with mockery of mere belief, and then afterwards to be ordered to believe many fabulous and absurd myths impossible to prove true".[38] Though he accorded the Platonists a place of privilege, Augustine rebuked them because, knowing the goal to seek, they had ignored the path which leads to it: the Word made flesh.[39] The Bishop of Hippo succeeded in producing the first great synthesis of philosophy and theology, embracing cur-

[38] SAINT AUGUSTINE, *Confessions*, VI, 5, 7: *CCL* 27, 77-78.
[39] Cf. *ibid.*, VII, 9, 13-14: *CCL* 27, 101-102.

rents of thought both Greek and Latin. In him too the great unity of knowledge, grounded in the thought of the Bible, was both confirmed and sustained by a depth of speculative thinking. The synthesis devised by Saint Augustine remained for centuries the most exalted form of philosophical and theological speculation known to the West. Reinforced by his personal story and sustained by a wonderful holiness of life, he could also introduce into his works a range of material which, drawing on experience, was a prelude to future developments in different currents of philosophy.

41.   The ways in which the Fathers of East and West engaged the philosophical schools were, therefore, quite different. This does not mean that they identified the content of their message with the systems to which they referred. Consider Tertullian's question: "What does Athens have in common with Jerusalem? The Academy with the Church?".[40] This clearly indicates the critical consciousness with which Christian thinkers from the first confronted the problem of the relationship between faith and philosophy, viewing it comprehensively with both its positive aspects and its limitations. They were not naive thinkers. Precisely because they were intense in living faith's content they were able to reach the deepest forms of speculation. It is therefore minimal-

[40] *De Praescriptione Haereticorum,* VII, 9: *SC* 46, 98: "*Quid ergo Athenis et Hierosolymis? Quid academiae et ecclesiae?*".

izing and mistaken to restrict their work simply to the transposition of the truths of faith into philosophical categories. They did much more. In fact they succeeded in disclosing completely all that remained implicit and preliminary in the thinking of the great philosophers of antiquity.[41] As I have noted, theirs was the task of showing how reason, freed from external constraints, could find its way out of the blind alley of myth and open itself to the transcendent in a more appropriate way. Purified and rightly tuned, therefore, reason could rise to the higher planes of thought, providing a solid foundation for the perception of being, of the transcendent and of the absolute.

It is here that we see the originality of what the Fathers accomplished. They fully welcomed reason which was open to the absolute, and they infused it with the richness drawn from Revelation. This was more than a meeting of cultures, with one culture perhaps succumbing to the fascination of the other. It happened rather in the depths of human souls, and it was a meeting of creature and Creator. Surpassing the goal towards which it unwittingly tended by dint of its nature, reason attained the supreme good and ultimate truth in the person of the Word made flesh. Faced with the various philosophies, the Fathers were not afraid to acknowledge those elements in

[41] Cf. CONGREGATION FOR CATHOLIC EDUCATION, Instruction on the Study of the Fathers of the Church in Priestly Formation (10 November 1989), 25: *AAS* 82 (1990), 617-618.

them that were consonant with Revelation and those that were not. Recognition of the points of convergence did not blind them to the points of divergence.

42. In Scholastic theology, the role of philosophically trained reason becomes even more conspicuous under the impulse of Saint Anselm's interpretation of the *intellectus fidei*. For the saintly Archbishop of Canterbury the priority of faith is not in competition with the search which is proper to reason. Reason in fact is not asked to pass judgement on the contents of faith, something of which it would be incapable, since this is not its function. Its function is rather to find meaning, to discover explanations which might allow everyone to come to a certain understanding of the contents of faith. Saint Anselm underscores the fact that the intellect must seek that which it loves: the more it loves, the more it desires to know. Whoever lives for the truth is reaching for a form of knowledge which is fired more and more with love for what it knows, while having to admit that it has not yet attained what it desires: "To see you was I conceived; and I have yet to conceive that for which I was conceived (*Ad te videndum factus sum; et nondum feci propter quod factus sum*)".[42] The desire for truth, therefore, spurs reason always to go further; indeed, it is as if reason were overwhelmed

---

[42] SAINT ANSELM, *Proslogion*, 1: PL 158, 226.

to see that it can always go beyond what it has already achieved. It is at this point, though, that reason can learn where its path will lead in the end: "I think that whoever investigates something incomprehensible should be satisfied if, by way of reasoning, he reaches a quite certain perception of its reality, even if his intellect cannot penetrate its mode of being... But is there anything so incomprehensible and ineffable as that which is above all things? Therefore, if that which until now has been a matter of debate concerning the highest essence has been established on the basis of due reasoning, then the foundation of one's certainty is not shaken in the least if the intellect cannot penetrate it in a way that allows clear formulation. If prior thought has concluded rationally that one cannot comprehend (*rationabiliter comprehendit incomprehensibile esse*) how supernal wisdom knows its own accomplishments..., who then will explain how this same wisdom, of which the human being can know nothing or next to nothing, is to be known and expressed?".[43]

The fundamental harmony between the knowledge of faith and the knowledge of philosophy is once again confirmed. Faith asks that its object be understood with the help of reason; and at the summit of its searching reason acknowledges that it cannot do without what faith presents.

---

[43] IDEM, *Monologion,* 64: PL 158, 210.

43. A quite special place in this long development belongs to Saint Thomas, not only because of what he taught but also because of the dialogue which he undertook with the Arab and Jewish thought of his time. In an age when Christian thinkers were rediscovering the treasures of ancient philosophy, and more particularly of Aristotle, Thomas had the great merit of giving pride of place to the harmony which exists between faith and reason. Both the light of reason and the light of faith come from God, he argued; hence there can be no contradiction between them.[44]

More radically, Thomas recognized that nature, philosophy's proper concern, could contribute to the understanding of divine Revelation. Faith therefore has no fear of reason, but seeks it out and has trust in it. Just as grace builds on nature and brings it to fulfilment,[45] so faith builds upon and perfects reason. Illumined by faith, reason is set free from the fragility and limitations deriving from the disobedience of sin and finds the strength required to rise to the knowledge of the Triune God. Although he made much of the supernatural character of faith, the Angelic Doctor did not overlook the importance of its rea-

[44] Cf. *Summa contra Gentiles,* I, 7.
[45] Cf. *Summa Theologiae,* I, 1, 8 ad 2: "*cum enim gratia non tollat naturam sed perficiat*".

sonableness; indeed he was able to plumb the depths and explain the meaning of this reasonableness. Faith is in a sense an "exercise of thought"; and human reason is neither annulled nor debased in assenting to the contents of faith, which are in any case attained by way of free and informed choice.[46]

This is why the Church has been justified in consistently proposing Saint Thomas as a master of thought and a model of the right way to do theology. In this connection, I would recall what my Predecessor, the Servant of God Paul VI, wrote on the occasion of the seventh centenary of the death of the Angelic Doctor: "Without doubt, Thomas possessed supremely the courage of the truth, a freedom of spirit in confronting new problems, the intellectual honesty of those who allow Christianity to be contaminated neither by secular philosophy nor by a prejudiced rejection of it. He passed therefore into the history of Christian thought as a pioneer of the new path of philosophy and universal culture. The key point and almost the kernel of the solution which, with all the brilliance of his prophetic intuition, he gave to the new encounter of faith and reason was a reconciliation between the secularity of the world and the radicality of the Gospel, thus avoiding the unnatural tendency to negate the world and its values while at the same

---

[46] Cf. JOHN PAUL II, Address to the Participants at the IX International Thomistic Congress (29 September 1990): *Insegnamenti*, XIII, 2 (1990), 770-771.

time keeping faith with the supreme and inexorable demands of the supernatural order".[47]

44.   Another of the great insights of Saint Thomas was his perception of the role of the Holy Spirit in the process by which knowledge matures into wisdom. From the first pages of his *Summa Theologiae*,[48] Aquinas was keen to show the primacy of the wisdom which is the gift of the Holy Spirit and which opens the way to a knowledge of divine realities. His theology allows us to understand what is distinctive of wisdom in its close link with faith and knowledge of the divine. This wisdom comes to know by way of connaturality; it presupposes faith and eventually formulates its right judgement on the basis of the truth of faith itself: "The wisdom named among the gifts of the Holy Spirit is distinct from the wisdom found among the intellectual virtues. This second wisdom is acquired through study, but the first 'comes from on high', as Saint James puts it. This also distinguishes it from faith, since faith accepts divine truth as it is. But the gift of wisdom enables judgement according to divine truth".[49]

Yet the priority accorded this wisdom does not lead the Angelic Doctor to overlook the pres-

[47] Apostolic Letter *Lumen Ecclesiae* (20 November 1974), 8: *AAS* 66 (1974), 680.
[48] Cf. I, 1, 6: "*Praeterea, haec doctrina per studium acquiritur. Sapientia autem per infusionem habetur, unde inter septem dona Spiritus Sancti connumeratur*".
[49] *Ibid.*, II-II, 45, 1 ad 2; cf. also II-II, 45, 2.

ence of two other complementary forms of wisdom—*philosophical* wisdom, which is based upon the capacity of the intellect, for all its natural limitations, to explore reality, and *theological* wisdom, which is based upon Revelation and which explores the contents of faith, entering the very mystery of God.

Profoundly convinced that "whatever its source, truth is of the Holy Spirit" (*omne verum a quocumque dicatur a Spiritu Sancto est*) [50] Saint Thomas was impartial in his love of truth. He sought truth wherever it might be found and gave consummate demonstration of its universality. In him, the Church's Magisterium has seen and recognized the passion for truth; and, precisely because it stays consistently within the horizon of universal, objective and transcendent truth, his thought scales "heights unthinkable to human intelligence".[51] Rightly, then, he may be called an "apostle of the truth".[52] Looking unreservedly to truth, the realism of Thomas could recognize the objectivity of truth and produce not merely a philosophy of "what seems to be" but a philosophy of "what is".

[50] *Ibid.*, I-II, 109, 1 ad 1, which echoes the well known phrase of the *Ambrosiaster, In Prima Cor* 12:3: *PL* 17, 258.

[51] Leo XIII, Encyclical Letter *Aeterni Patris* (4 August 1879): *ASS* 11 (1878-79), 109.

[52] Paul VI, Apostolic Letter *Lumen Ecclesiae* (20 November 1974), 8: *AAS* 66 (1974), 683.

45. With the rise of the first universities, theology came more directly into contact with other forms of learning and scientific research. Although they insisted upon the organic link between theology and philosophy, Saint Albert the Great and Saint Thomas were the first to recognize the autonomy which philosophy and the sciences needed if they were to perform well in their respective fields of research. From the late Medieval period onwards, however, the legitimate distinction between the two forms of learning became more and more a fateful separation. As a result of the exaggerated rationalism of certain thinkers, positions grew more radical and there emerged eventually a philosophy which was separate from and absolutely independent of the contents of faith. Another of the many consequences of this separation was an ever deeper mistrust with regard to reason itself. In a spirit both sceptical and agnostic, some began to voice a general mistrust, which led some to focus more on faith and others to deny its rationality altogether.

In short, what for Patristic and Medieval thought was in both theory and practice a profound unity, producing knowledge capable of reaching the highest forms of speculation, was destroyed by systems which espoused the cause of rational knowledge sundered from faith and meant to take the place of faith.

46.   The more influential of these radical positions are well known and high in profile, especially in the history of the West. It is not too much to claim that the development of a good part of modern philosophy has seen it move further and further away from Christian Revelation, to the point of setting itself quite explicitly in opposition. This process reached its apogee in the last century. Some representatives of idealism sought in various ways to transform faith and its contents, even the mystery of the Death and Resurrection of Jesus, into dialectical structures which could be grasped by reason. Opposed to this kind of thinking were various forms of atheistic humanism, expressed in philosophical terms, which regarded faith as alienating and damaging to the development of a full rationality. They did not hesitate to present themselves as new religions serving as a basis for projects which, on the political and social plane, gave rise to totalitarian systems which have been disastrous for humanity.

In the field of scientific research, a positivistic mentality took hold which not only abandoned the Christian vision of the world, but more especially rejected every appeal to a metaphysical or moral vision. It follows that certain scientists, lacking any ethical point of reference, are in danger of putting at the centre of their concerns something other than the human person and the entirety of the person's life. Further still, some of these, sensing the opportunities of technological progress, seem to succumb not only to a market-based logic, but also to the temptation of a quasi-divine power over nature and even over the human being.

As a result of the crisis of rationalism, what has appeared finally is *nihilism.* As a philosophy of nothingness, it has a certain attraction for people of our time. Its adherents claim that the search is an end in itself, without any hope or possibility of ever attaining the goal of truth. In the nihilist interpretation, life is no more than an occasion for sensations and experiences in which the ephemeral has pride of place. Nihilism is at the root of the widespread mentality which claims that a definitive commitment should no longer be made, because everything is fleeting and provisional.

47.   It should also be borne in mind that the role of philosophy itself has changed in modern culture. From universal wisdom and learning, it has been gradually reduced to one of the many fields of human knowing; indeed in some ways it has been consigned to a wholly marginal role. Other forms of rationality have acquired an ever higher profile, making philosophical learning appear all the more peripheral. These forms of rationality are directed not towards the contemplation of truth and the search for the ultimate goal and meaning of life; but instead, as "instrumental reason", they are directed—actually or potential-

ly—towards the promotion of utilitarian ends, towards enjoyment or power.

In my first Encyclical Letter I stressed the danger of absolutizing such an approach when I wrote: "The man of today seems ever to be under threat from what he produces, that is to say from the result of the work of his hands and, even more so, of the work of his intellect and the tendencies of his will. All too soon, and often in an unforeseeable way, what this manifold activity of man yields is not only subject to 'alienation', in the sense that it is simply taken away from the person who produces it, but rather it turns against man himself, at least in part, through the indirect consequences of its effects returning on himself. It is or can be directed against him. This seems to make up the main chapter of the drama of present-day human existence in its broadest and universal dimension. Man therefore lives increasingly in fear. He is afraid of what he produces—not all of it, of course, or even most of it, but part of it and precisely that part that contains a special share of his genius and initiative—can radically turn against himself".[53]

In the wake of these cultural shifts, some philosophers have abandoned the search for truth in itself and made their sole aim the attainment of a subjective certainty or a pragmatic sense of

[53] Encyclical Letter *Redemptor Hominis* (4 March 1979), 15: *AAS* 71 (1979), 286.

utility. This in turn has obscured the true dignity of reason, which is no longer equipped to know the truth and to seek the absolute.

48.   This rapid survey of the history of philosophy, then, reveals a growing separation between faith and philosophical reason. Yet closer scrutiny shows that even in the philosophical thinking of those who helped drive faith and reason further apart there are found at times precious and seminal insights which, if pursued and developed with mind and heart rightly tuned, can lead to the discovery of truth's way. Such insights are found, for instance, in penetrating analyses of perception and experience, of the imaginary and the unconscious, of personhood and intersubjectivity, of freedom and values, of time and history. The theme of death as well can become for all thinkers an incisive appeal to seek within themselves the true meaning of their own life. But this does not mean that the link between faith and reason as it now stands does not need to be carefully examined, because each without the other is impoverished and enfeebled. Deprived of what Revelation offers, reason has taken sidetracks which expose it to the danger of losing sight of its final goal. Deprived of reason, faith has stressed feeling and experience, and so run the risk of no longer being a universal proposition. It is an illusion to think that faith, tied to weak reasoning, might be more penetrating; on the contrary, faith then runs the grave risk of

withering into myth or superstition. By the same token, reason which is unrelated to an adult faith is not prompted to turn its gaze to the newness and radicality of being.

This is why I make this strong and insistent appeal—not, I trust, untimely—that faith and philosophy recover the profound unity which allows them to stand in harmony with their nature without compromising their mutual autonomy. The *parrhesia* of faith must be matched by the boldness of reason.

CHAPTER V

THE MAGISTERIUM'S INTERVENTIONS IN PHILOSOPHICAL MATTERS

The Magisterium's discernment as diakonia of the truth

49.   The Church has no philosophy of her own nor does she canonize any one particular philosophy in preference to others.[54] The underlying reason for this reluctance is that, even when it engages theology, philosophy must remain faithful to its own principles and methods. Otherwise there would be no guarantee that it would remain oriented to truth and that it was moving towards truth by way of a process governed by reason. A philosophy which did not proceed in the light of reason according to its own principles and methods would serve little purpose. At the deepest level, the autonomy which philosophy enjoys is rooted in the fact that reason is by its nature oriented to truth and is equipped moreover with the means necessary to arrive at truth. A philosophy conscious of this as its "constitutive status" cannot but respect the demands and the data of revealed truth.

[54] Cf. Pius XII, Encyclical Letter *Humani Generis* (12 August 1950): *AAS* 42 (1950), 566.

Yet history shows that philosophy—especially modern philosophy—has taken wrong turns and fallen into error. It is neither the task nor the competence of the Magisterium to intervene in order to make good the lacunas of deficient philosophical discourse. Rather, it is the Magisterium's duty to respond clearly and strongly when controversial philosophical opinions threaten right understanding of what has been revealed, and when false and partial theories which sow the seed of serious error, confusing the pure and simple faith of the People of God, begin to spread more widely.

50. In the light of faith, therefore, the Church's Magisterium can and must authoritatively exercise a critical discernment of opinions and philosophies which contradict Christian doctrine.[55] It is the task of the Magisterium in the first place to indicate which philosophical presuppositions and conclusions are incompatible with revealed truth, thus articulating the demands which faith's point of view makes of philosophy. Moreover, as philosophical learning has developed, different schools of thought have emerged. This pluralism also imposes upon the Magisterium the responsibility of expressing a judgement as to whether or not the basic tenets of these different

[55] Cf. FIRST VATICAN ECUMENICAL COUNCIL, Dogmatic Constitution on the Church of Christ *Pastor Aeternus: DS* 3070; SECOND VATICAN ECUMENICAL COUNCIL, Dogmatic Constitution on the Church *Lumen Gentium,* 25 c.

schools are compatible with the demands of the word of God and theological enquiry.

It is the Church's duty to indicate the elements in a philosophical system which are incompatible with her own faith. In fact, many philosophical opinions—concerning God, the human being, human freedom and ethical behaviour—engage the Church directly, because they touch on the revealed truth of which she is the guardian. In making this discernment, we Bishops have the duty to be "witnesses to the truth", fulfilling a humble but tenacious ministry of service which every philosopher should appreciate, a service in favour of *recta ratio*, or of reason reflecting rightly upon what is true.

51.   This discernment, however, should not be seen as primarily negative, as if the Magisterium intended to abolish or limit any possible mediation. On the contrary, the Magisterium's interventions are intended above all to prompt, promote and encourage philosophical enquiry. Besides, philosophers are the first to understand the need for self-criticism, the correction of errors and the extension of the too restricted terms in which their thinking has been framed. In particular, it is necessary to keep in mind the unity of truth, even if its formulations are shaped by history and produced by human reason wounded and weakened by sin. This is why no historical form of philosophy can legitimately claim to embrace the totality of truth, nor to be the complete explana-

tion of the human being, of the world and of the human being's relationship with God.

Today, then, with the proliferation of systems, methods, concepts and philosophical theses which are often extremely complex, the need for a critical discernment in the light of faith becomes more urgent, even if it remains a daunting task. Given all of reason's inherent and historical limitations, it is difficult enough to recognize the inalienable powers proper to it; but it is still more difficult at times to discern in specific philosophical claims what is valid and fruitful from faith's point of view and what is mistaken or dangerous. Yet the Church knows that "the treasures of wisdom and knowledge" are hidden in Christ (*Col* 2:3) and therefore intervenes in order to stimulate philosophical enquiry, lest it stray from the path which leads to recognition of the mystery.

52.   It is not only in recent times that the Magisterium of the Church has intervened to make its mind known with regard to particular philosophical teachings. It is enough to recall, by way of example, the pronouncements made through the centuries concerning theories which argued in favour of the pre-existence of the soul,[56] or concerning the different forms of idolatry and esoteric superstition found in astrological speculations,[57] without forgetting the more system-

[56] Cf. SYNOD OF CONSTANTINOPLE, *DS* 403.
[57] Cf. COUNCIL OF TOLEDO I, *DS* 205; COUNCIL OF BRAGA I, *DS* 459-460; SIXTUS V, Bull *Coeli et Terrae Creator*

atic pronouncements against certain claims of Latin Averroism which were incompatible with the Christian faith.[58]

If the Magisterium has spoken out more frequently since the middle of the last century, it is because in that period not a few Catholics felt it their duty to counter various streams of modern thought with a philosophy of their own. At this point, the Magisterium of the Church was obliged to be vigilant lest these philosophies developed in ways which were themselves erroneous and negative. The censures were delivered evenhandedly: on the one hand, *fideism*[59] and *radical traditionalism*,[60] for their distrust of reason's natural capacities, and, on the other, *rationalism*[61] and *ontologism*[62] because they attributed to natural reason a knowledge which only the light of faith could confer. The positive elements of this de-

(5 January 1586): *Bullarium Romanum* 4/4, Rome 1747, 176-179; URBAN VIII, *Inscrutabilis Iudiciorum* (1 April 1631): *Bullarium Romanum* 6/1, Rome 1758, 268-270.

[58] Cf. ECUMENICAL COUNCIL OF VIENNE, Decree *Fidei Catholicae, DS* 902; FIFTH LATERAN ECUMENICAL COUNCIL, Bull *Apostoli Regiminis, DS* 1440.

[59] Cf. *Theses a Ludovico Eugenio Bautain iussu sui Episcopi subscriptae* (8 September 1840), *DS* 2751-2756; *Theses a Ludovico Eugenio Bautain ex mandato S. Cong. Episcoporum et Religiosorum subscriptae* (26 April 1844), *DS* 2765-2769.

[60] Cf. SACRED CONGREGATION OF THE INDEX, Decree *Theses contra Traditionalismum Augustini Bonnetty* (11 June 1855), *DS* 2811-2814.

[61] Cf. PIUS IX, Brief *Eximiam Tuam* (15 June 1857), *DS* 2828-2831; Brief *Gravissimas Inter* (11 December 1862), *DS* 2850-2861.

[62] Cf. SACRED CONGREGATION OF THE HOLY OFFICE, Decree *Errores Ontologistarum* (18 September 1861), *DS* 2841-2847.

bate were assembled in the Dogmatic Constitution *Dei Filius*, in which for the first time an Ecumenical Council—in this case, the First Vatican Council—pronounced solemnly on the relationship between reason and faith. The teaching contained in this document strongly and positively marked the philosophical research of many believers and remains today a standard reference-point for correct and coherent Christian thinking in this regard.

53. The Magisterium's pronouncements have been concerned less with individual philosophical theses than with the need for rational and hence ultimately philosophical knowledge for the understanding of faith. In synthesizing and solemnly reaffirming the teachings constantly proposed to the faithful by the ordinary Papal Magisterium, the First Vatican Council showed how inseparable and at the same time how distinct were faith and reason, Revelation and natural knowledge of God. The Council began with the basic criterion, presupposed by Revelation itself, of the natural knowability of the existence of God, the beginning and end of all things,[63] and concluded with the solemn assertion quoted earlier: "There are two orders of knowledge, distinct not only in their point of departure, but also in their ob-

[63] Cf. FIRST VATICAN ECUMENICAL COUNCIL, Dogmatic Constitution on the Catholic Faith *Dei Filius,* II: *DS* 3004; and Canon 2, 1: *DS* 3026.

ject".[64] Against all forms of rationalism, then, there was a need to affirm the distinction between the mysteries of faith and the findings of philosophy, and the transcendence and precedence of the mysteries of faith over the findings of philosophy. Against the temptations of fideism, however, it was necessary to stress the unity of truth and thus the positive contribution which rational knowledge can and must make to faith's knowledge: "Even if faith is superior to reason there can never be a true divergence between faith and reason, since the same God who reveals the mysteries and bestows the gift of faith has also placed in the human spirit the light of reason. This God could not deny himself, nor could the truth ever contradict the truth".[65]

54. In our own century too the Magisterium has revisited the theme on a number of occasions, warning against the lure of rationalism. Here the pronouncements of Pope Saint Pius X are pertinent, stressing as they did that at the basis of Modernism were philosophical claims which were phenomenist, agnostic and immanentist.[66] Nor can the importance of the Catholic re-

[64] *Ibid.,* IV: *DS* 3015, cited in SECOND VATICAN ECUMENICAL COUNCIL, Pastoral Constitution on the Church in the Modern World *Gaudium et Spes,* 59.

[65] FIRST VATICAN ECUMENICAL COUNCIL, Dogmatic Constitution on the Catholic Faith *Dei Filius,* IV: *DS* 3017.

[66] Cf. Encyclical Letter *Pascendi Dominici Gregis* (8 September 1907): *ASS* 40 (1907), 596-597.

jection of Marxist philosophy and atheistic Communism be forgotten.[67]

Later, in his Encyclical Letter *Humani Generis*, Pope Pius XII warned against mistaken interpretations linked to evolutionism, existentialism and historicism. He made it clear that these theories had not been proposed and developed by theologians, but had their origins "outside the sheepfold of Christ".[68] He added, however, that errors of this kind should not simply be rejected but should be examined critically: "Catholic theologians and philosophers, whose grave duty it is to defend natural and supernatural truth and instill it in human hearts, cannot afford to ignore these more or less erroneous opinions. Rather they must come to understand these theories well, not only because diseases are properly treated only if rightly diagnosed and because even in these false theories some truth is found at times, but because in the end these theories provoke a more discriminating discussion and evaluation of philosophical and theological truths".[69]

In accomplishing its specific task in service of the Roman Pontiff's universal Magisterium,[70] the

[67] Cf. Pius XI, Encyclical Letter *Divini Redemptoris* (19 March 1937): *AAS* 29 (1937), 65-106.

[68] Encyclical Letter *Humani Generis* (12 August 1950): *AAS* 42 (1950), 562-563.

[69] *Ibid., loc. cit.*, 563-564.

[70] Cf. John Paul II, Apostolic Constitution *Pastor Bonus* (28 June 1988), Arts. 48-49: *AAS* 80 (1988), 873; Congregation for the Doctrine of the Faith, Instruction on the Ecclesial Vocation of the Theologian *Donum Veritatis* (24 May 1990), 18: *AAS* 82 (1990), 1558.

Congregation for the Doctrine of Faith has more recently had to intervene to re-emphasize the danger of an uncritical adoption by some liberation theologians of opinions and methods drawn from Marxism.[71]

In the past, then, the Magisterium has on different occasions and in different ways offered its discernment in philosophical matters. My revered Predecessors have thus made an invaluable contribution which must not be forgotten.

55. Surveying the situation today, we see that the problems of other times have returned, but in a new key. It is no longer a matter of questions of interest only to certain individuals and groups, but convictions so widespread that they have become to some extent the common mind. An example of this is the deep-seated distrust of reason which has surfaced in the most recent developments of much of philosophical research, to the point where there is talk at times of "the end of metaphysics". Philosophy is expected to rest content with more modest tasks such as the simple interpretation of facts or an enquiry into restricted fields of human knowing or its structures.

In theology too the temptations of other times have reappeared. In some contemporary theologies, for instance, a certain *rationalism* is gaining ground, especially when opinions thought

---

[71] Cf. Instruction on Certain Aspects of the "Theology of Liberation" *Libertatis Nuntius* (6 August 1984), VII-X: *AAS* 76 (1984), 890-903.

to be philosophically well founded are taken as normative for theological research. This happens particularly when theologians, through lack of philosophical competence, allow themselves to be swayed uncritically by assertions which have become part of current parlance and culture but which are poorly grounded in reason.[72]

There are also signs of a resurgence of *fideism*, which fails to recognize the importance of rational knowledge and philosophical discourse for the understanding of faith, indeed for the very possibility of belief in God. One currently widespread symptom of this fideistic tendency is a "biblicism" which tends to make the reading and exegesis of Sacred Scripture the sole criterion of truth. In consequence, the word of God is identified with Sacred Scripture alone, thus eliminating the doctrine of the Church which the Sec-

---

[72] In language as clear as it is authoritative, the First Vatican Council condemned this error, affirming on the one hand that "as regards this faith..., the Catholic Church professes that it is a supernatural virtue by means of which, under divine inspiration and with the help of grace, we believe to be true the things revealed by God, not because of the intrinsic truth of the things perceived by the natural light of reason, but because of the authority of God himself, who reveals them and who can neither deceive nor be deceived": Dogmatic Constitution *Dei Filius,* III: *DS* 3008, and Canon 3, 2: *DS* 3032. On the other hand, the Council declared that reason is never "able to penetrate [these mysteries] as it does the truths which are its proper object": *ibid.,* IV: *DS* 3016. It then drew a practical conclusion: "The Christian faithful not only have no right to defend as legitimate scientific conclusions opinions which are contrary to the doctrine of the faith, particularly if condemned by the Church, but they are strictly obliged to regard them as errors which have no more than a fraudulent semblance of truth": *ibid.,* IV: *DS* 3018.

ond Vatican Council stressed quite specifically. Having recalled that the word of God is present in both Scripture and Tradition,[73] the Constitution *Dei Verbum* continues emphatically: "Sacred Tradition and Sacred Scripture comprise a single sacred deposit of the word of God entrusted to the Church. Embracing this deposit and united with their pastors, the People of God remain always faithful to the teaching of the Apostles".[74] Scripture, therefore, is not the Church's sole point of reference. The "supreme rule of her faith" [75] derives from the unity which the Spirit has created between Sacred Tradition, Sacred Scripture and the Magisterium of the Church in a reciprocity which means that none of the three can survive without the others.[76]

Moreover, one should not underestimate the danger inherent in seeking to derive the truth of Sacred Scripture from the use of one method alone, ignoring the need for a more comprehensive exegesis which enables the exegete, together with the whole Church, to arrive at the full sense of the texts. Those who devote themselves to the study of Sacred Scripture should always remember that the various hermeneutical approaches have their own philosophical underpinnings, which need to be carefully evaluated before they are applied to the sacred texts.

[73] Cf. Nos. 9-10.
[74] *Ibid.,* 10.
[75] *Ibid.,* 21.
[76] Cf. *ibid.,* 10.

Other modes of latent fideism appear in the scant consideration accorded to speculative theology, and in disdain for the classical philosophy from which the terms of both the understanding of faith and the actual formulation of dogma have been drawn. My revered Predecessor Pope Pius XII warned against such neglect of the philosophical tradition and against abandonment of the traditional terminology.[77]

56.   In brief, there are signs of a widespread distrust of universal and absolute statements, especially among those who think that truth is born of consensus and not of a consonance between intellect and objective reality. In a world subdivided into so many specialized fields, it is not hard to see how difficult it can be to acknowledge the full and ultimate meaning of life which has traditionally been the goal of philosophy. Nonetheless, in the light of faith which finds in Jesus Christ this ultimate meaning, I cannot but encourage philosophers—be they Christian or not—to trust in the power of human reason and not to set themselves goals that are too modest in their philosophizing. The lesson of history in this millennium now drawing to a close shows that this is the path to follow: it is necessary not to abandon the passion for ultimate truth, the eagerness to search for it or the audacity to forge new paths in the search. It is faith which stirs reason

[77] Cf. Encyclical Letter *Humani Generis* (12 August 1950): *AAS* 42 (1950), 565-567; 571-573.

to move beyond all isolation and willingly to run risks so that it may attain whatever is beautiful, good and true. Faith thus becomes the convinced and convincing advocate of reason.

The Church's interest in philosophy

57. Yet the Magisterium does more than point out the misperceptions and the mistakes of philosophical theories. With no less concern it has sought to stress the basic principles of a genuine renewal of philosophical enquiry, indicating as well particular paths to be taken. In this regard, Pope Leo XIII with his Encyclical Letter *Aeterni Patris* took a step of historic importance for the life of the Church, since it remains to this day the one papal document of such authority devoted entirely to philosophy. The great Pope revisited and developed the First Vatican Council's teaching on the relationship between faith and reason, showing how philosophical thinking contributes in fundamental ways to faith and theological learning.[78] More than a century later, many of the insights of his Encyclical Letter have lost none of their interest from either a practical or pedagogical point of view—most particularly, his insistence upon the incomparable value of the philosophy of Saint Thomas. A renewed insistence upon the thought of the Angelic Doctor

[78] Cf. Encyclical Letter *Aeterni Patris* (4 August 1879): *ASS* 11 (1878-1879), 97-115.

seemed to Pope Leo XIII the best way to recover the practice of a philosophy consonant with the demands of faith. "Just when Saint Thomas distinguishes perfectly between faith and reason", the Pope writes, "he unites them in bonds of mutual friendship, conceding to each its specific rights and to each its specific dignity".[79]

58. The positive results of the papal summons are well known. Studies of the thought of Saint Thomas and other Scholastic writers received new impetus. Historical studies flourished, resulting in a rediscovery of the riches of Medieval thought, which until then had been largely unknown; and there emerged new Thomistic schools. With the use of historical method, knowledge of the works of Saint Thomas increased greatly, and many scholars had courage enough to introduce the Thomistic tradition into the philosophical and theological discussions of the day. The most influential Catholic theologians of the present century, to whose thinking and research the Second Vatican Council was much indebted, were products of this revival of Thomistic philosophy. Throughout the twentieth century, the Church has been served by a powerful array of thinkers formed in the school of the Angelic Doctor.

59. Yet the Thomistic and neo-Thomistic revival was not the only sign of a resurgence of

[79] *Ibid., loc. cit.*, 109.

philosophical thought in culture of Christian inspiration. Earlier still, and parallel to Pope Leo's call, there had emerged a number of Catholic philosophers who, adopting more recent currents of thought and according to a specific method, produced philosophical works of great influence and lasting value. Some devised syntheses so remarkable that they stood comparison with the great systems of idealism. Others established the epistemological foundations for a new consideration of faith in the light of a renewed understanding of moral consciousness; others again produced a philosophy which, starting with an analysis of immanence, opened the way to the transcendent; and there were finally those who sought to combine the demands of faith with the perspective of phenomenological method. From different quarters, then, modes of philosophical speculation have continued to emerge and have sought to keep alive the great tradition of Christian thought which unites faith and reason.

60. The Second Vatican Council, for its part, offers a rich and fruitful teaching concerning philosophy. I cannot fail to note, especially in the context of this Encyclical Letter, that one chapter of the Constitution *Gaudium et Spes* amounts to a virtual compendium of the biblical anthropology from which philosophy too can draw inspiration. The chapter deals with the value of the human person created in the image of God, explains the dignity and superiority of the human being over

the rest of creation, and declares the transcendent capacity of human reason.[80] The problem of atheism is also dealt with in *Gaudium et Spes*, and the flaws of its philosophical vision are identified, especially in relation to the dignity and freedom of the human person.[81] There is no doubt that the climactic section of the chapter is profoundly significant for philosophy; and it was this which I took up in my first Encyclical Letter *Redemptor Hominis* and which serves as one of the constant reference-points of my teaching: "The truth is that only in the mystery of the Incarnate Word does the mystery of man take on light. For Adam, the first man, was a type of him who was to come, Christ the Lord. Christ, the new Adam, in the very revelation of the mystery of the Father and of his love, fully reveals man to himself and brings to light his most high calling".[82]

The Council also dealt with the study of philosophy required of candidates for the priesthood; and its recommendations have implications for Christian education as a whole. These are the Council's words: "The philosophical disciplines should be taught in such a way that students acquire in the first place a solid and harmonious knowledge of the human being, of the world and of God, based upon the philosophical heritage

---

[80] Cf. Nos. 14-15.

[81] Cf. *ibid.,* 20-21.

[82] *Ibid.,* 22; cf. JOHN PAUL II, Encyclical Letter *Redemptor Hominis* (4 March 1979), 8: *AAS* 71 (1979), 271-272.

which is enduringly valid, yet taking into account
currents of modern philosophy".[83]

These directives have been reiterated and developed in a number of other magisterial docu-
ments in order to guarantee a solid philosophical
formation, especially for those preparing for theological studies. I have myself emphasized several
times the importance of this philosophical formation for those who one day, in their pastoral life,
will have to address the aspirations of the contemporary world and understand the causes of
certain behaviour in order to respond in appropriate ways.[84]

61. If it has been necessary from time to time
to intervene on this question, to reiterate the value of the Angelic Doctor's insights and insist on
the study of his thought, this has been because
the Magisterium's directives have not always been
followed with the readiness one would wish. In

---

[83] Decree on Priestly Formation *Optatam Totius,* 15.

[84] Cf. Apostolic Constitution *Sapientia Christiana* (15 April
1979), Arts. 79-80: *AAS* 71 (1979), 495-496; Post-Synodal Apostolic Exhortation *Pastores Dabo Vobis* (25 March 1992), 52: *AAS*
84 (1992), 750-751. Cf. also various remarks on the philosophy
of Saint Thomas: Address to the International Pontifical Athenaeum "Angelicum" (17 November 1979): *Insegnamenti* II, 2 (1979),
1177-1189; Address to the Participants of the Eighth International Thomistic Congress (13 September 1980): *Insegnamenti* III, 2
(1980), 604-615; Address to the Participants at the International
Congress of the Saint Thomas Society on the Doctrine of the
Soul in Saint Thomas (4 January 1986): *Insegnamenti* IX, 1
(1986), 18-24. Also the SACRED CONGREGATION FOR CATHO-
LIC EDUCATION, *Ratio Fundamentalis Institutionis Sacerdotalis* (6
January 1970), 70-75: *AAS* 62 (1970), 366-368; Decree *Sacra
Theologia* (20 January 1972): *AAS* 64 (1972), 583-586.

the years after the Second Vatican Council, many Catholic faculties were in some ways impoverished by a diminished sense of the importance of the study not just of Scholastic philosophy but more generally of the study of philosophy itself. I cannot fail to note with surprise and displeasure that this lack of interest in the study of philosophy is shared by not a few theologians.

There are various reasons for this disenchantment. First, there is the distrust of reason found in much contemporary philosophy, which has largely abandoned metaphysical study of the ultimate human questions in order to concentrate upon problems which are more detailed and restricted, at times even purely formal. Another reason, it should be said, is the misunderstanding which has arisen especially with regard to the "human sciences". On a number of occasions, the Second Vatican Council stressed the positive value of scientific research for a deeper knowledge of the mystery of the human being.[85] But the invitation addressed to theologians to engage the human sciences and apply them properly in their enquiries should not be interpreted as an implicit authorization to marginalize philosophy or to put something else in its place in pastoral formation and in the *praeparatio fidei.* A further factor is the renewed interest in the inculturation of faith. The life of the young Churches in par-

[85] Cf. Pastoral Constitution on the Church in the Modern World *Gaudium et Spes,* 57; 62.

ticular has brought to light, together with sophisticated modes of thinking, an array of expressions of popular wisdom; and this constitutes a genuine cultural wealth of traditions. Yet the study of traditional ways must go hand in hand with philosophical enquiry, an enquiry which will allow the positive traits of popular wisdom to emerge and forge the necessary link with the proclamation of the Gospel.[86]

62.   I wish to repeat clearly that the study of philosophy is fundamental and indispensable to the structure of theological studies and to the formation of candidates for the priesthood. It is not by chance that the curriculum of theological studies is preceded by a time of special study of philosophy. This decision, confirmed by the Fifth Lateran Council,[87] is rooted in the experience which matured through the Middle Ages, when the importance of a constructive harmony of philosophical and theological learning emerged. This ordering of studies influenced, promoted and enabled much of the development of modern philosophy, albeit indirectly. One telling example of this is the influence of the *Disputationes Metaphysicae* of Francisco Suárez, which found its way even into the Lutheran universities of Germany. Conversely, the dismantling of this arrangement

[86] Cf. *ibid.,* 44.
[87] Cf. FIFTH LATERAN ECUMENICAL COUNCIL, Bull *Apostolici Regimini Sollicitudo*, Session VIII: *Conciliorum Oecumenicorum Decreta*, 1991, 605-606.

has created serious gaps in both priestly formation and theological research. Consider, for instance, the disregard of modern thought and culture which has led either to a refusal of any kind of dialogue or to an indiscriminate acceptance of any kind of philosophy.

I trust most sincerely that these difficulties will be overcome by an intelligent philosophical and theological formation, which must never be lacking in the Church.

63.   For the reasons suggested here, it has seemed to me urgent to re-emphasize with this Encyclical Letter the Church's intense interest in philosophy—indeed the intimate bond which ties theological work to the philosophical search for truth. From this comes the Magisterium's duty to discern and promote philosophical thinking which is not at odds with faith. It is my task to state principles and criteria which in my judgement are necessary in order to restore a harmonious and creative relationship between theology and philosophy. In the light of these principles and criteria, it will be possible to discern with greater clarity what link, if any, theology should forge with the different philosophical opinions or systems which the world of today presents.

CHAPTER VI

THE INTERACTION
BETWEEN PHILOSOPHY AND THEOLOGY

*The knowledge of faith and the demands
of philosophical reason*

64.   The word of God is addressed to all people, in every age and in every part of the world; and the human being is by nature a philosopher. As a reflective and scientific elaboration of the understanding of God's word in the light of faith, theology for its part must relate, in some of its procedures and in the performance of its specific tasks, to the philosophies which have been developed through the ages. I have no wish to direct theologians to particular methods, since that is not the competence of the Magisterium. I wish instead to recall some specific tasks of theology which, by the very nature of the revealed word, demand recourse to philosophical enquiry.

65.   Theology is structured as an understanding of faith in the light of a twofold methodological principle: the *auditus fidei* and the *intellectus fidei*. With the first, theology makes its own the content of Revelation as this has been gradually expounded in Sacred Tradition, Sacred Scripture

and the Church's living Magisterium.[88] With the second, theology seeks to respond through speculative enquiry to the specific demands of disciplined thought.

Philosophy contributes specifically to theology in preparing for a correct *auditus fidei* with its study of the structure of knowledge and personal communication, especially the various forms and functions of language. No less important is philosophy's contribution to a more coherent understanding of Church Tradition, the pronouncements of the Magisterium and the teaching of the great masters of theology, who often adopt concepts and thought-forms drawn from a particular philosophical tradition. In this case, the theologian is summoned not only to explain the concepts and terms used by the Church in her thinking and the development of her teaching, but also to know in depth the philosophical systems which may have influenced those concepts and terms, in order to formulate correct and consistent interpretations of them.

66.   With regard to the *intellectus fidei*, a prime consideration must be that divine Truth "proposed to us in the Sacred Scriptures and rightly interpreted by the Church's teaching" [89] enjoys an innate intelligibility, so logically consistent that it

[88] Cf. SECOND VATICAN ECUMENICAL COUNCIL, Dogmatic Constitution on Divine Revelation *Dei Verbum*, 10.

[89] SAINT THOMAS AQUINAS, *Summa Theologiae*, II-II, 5, 3 ad 2.

stands as an authentic body of knowledge. The *intellectus fidei* expounds this truth, not only in grasping the logical and conceptual structure of the propositions in which the Church's teaching is framed, but also, indeed primarily, in bringing to light the salvific meaning of these propositions for the individual and for humanity. From the sum of these propositions, the believer comes to know the history of salvation, which culminates in the person of Jesus Christ and in his Paschal Mystery. Believers then share in this mystery by their assent of faith.

For its part, *dogmatic theology* must be able to articulate the universal meaning of the mystery of the One and Triune God and of the economy of salvation, both as a narrative and, above all, in the form of argument. It must do so, in other words, through concepts formulated in a critical and universally communicable way. Without philosophy's contribution, it would in fact be impossible to discuss theological issues such as, for example, the use of language to speak about God, the personal relations within the Trinity, God's creative activity in the world, the relationship between God and man, or Christ's identity as true God and true man. This is no less true of the different themes of moral theology, which employ concepts such as the moral law, conscience, freedom, personal responsibility and guilt, which are in part defined by philosophical ethics.

It is necessary therefore that the mind of the believer acquire a natural, consistent and true knowledge of created realities—the world and man himself—which are also the object of divine Revelation. Still more, reason must be able to articulate this knowledge in concept and argument. Speculative dogmatic theology thus presupposes and implies a philosophy of the human being, the world and, more radically, of being, which has objective truth as its foundation.

67.   With its specific character as a discipline charged with giving an account of faith (cf. *1 Pet* 3:15), the concern of *fundamental theology* will be to justify and expound the relationship between faith and philosophical thought. Recalling the teaching of Saint Paul (cf. *Rom* 1:19-20), the First Vatican Council pointed to the existence of truths which are naturally, and thus philosophically, knowable; and an acceptance of God's Revelation necessarily presupposes knowledge of these truths. In studying Revelation and its credibility, as well as the corresponding act of faith, fundamental theology should show how, in the light of the knowledge conferred by faith, there emerge certain truths which reason, from its own independent enquiry, already perceives. Revelation endows these truths with their fullest meaning, directing them towards the richness of the revealed mystery in which they find their ultimate purpose. Consider, for example, the natural knowledge of God, the possibility of distinguishing divine Revelation from other phenomena or the recognition of its credibility, the capacity of hu-

man language to speak in a true and meaningful way even of things which transcend all human experience. From all these truths, the mind is led to acknowledge the existence of a truly propaedeutic path to faith, one which can lead to the acceptance of Revelation without in any way compromising the principles and autonomy of the mind itself.[90]

Similarly, fundamental theology should demonstrate the profound compatibility that exists between faith and its need to find expression by way of human reason fully free to give its assent. Faith will thus be able "to show fully the path to reason in a sincere search for the truth. Although faith, a gift of God, is not based on reason, it can certainly not dispense with it. At the same time, it becomes apparent that reason needs to be reinforced by faith, in order to discover horizons it cannot reach on its own".[91]

68.   *Moral theology* has perhaps an even greater need of philosophy's contribution. In the New Testament, human life is much less governed by prescriptions than in the Old Testament. Life in

[90] "The search for the conditions in which man on his own initiative asks the first basic questions about the meaning of life, the purpose he wishes to give it and what awaits him after death constitutes the necessary preamble to fundamental theology, so that today too, faith can fully show the way to reason in a sincere search for the truth": JOHN PAUL II, *Letter to Participants in the International Congress of Fundamental Theology on the 125th Anniversary of "Dei Filius"* (30 September 1995), 4: *L'Osservatore Romano*, 3 October 1995, 8.
[91] *Ibid.*

the Spirit leads believers to a freedom and responsibility which surpass the Law. Yet the Gospel and the Apostolic writings still set forth both general principles of Christian conduct and specific teachings and precepts. In order to apply these to the particular circumstances of individual and communal life, Christians must be able fully to engage their conscience and the power of their reason. In other words, moral theology requires a sound philosophical vision of human nature and society, as well as of the general principles of ethical decision-making.

69.   It might be objected that the theologian should nowadays rely less on philosophy than on the help of other kinds of human knowledge, such as history and above all the sciences, the extraordinary advances of which in recent times stir such admiration. Others, more alert to the link between faith and culture, claim that theology should look more to the wisdom contained in peoples' traditions than to a philosophy of Greek and Eurocentric provenance. Others still, prompted by a mistaken notion of cultural pluralism, simply deny the universal value of the Church's philosophical heritage.

There is some truth in these claims which are acknowledged in the teaching of the Council.[92]

[92] Cf. SECOND VATICAN ECUMENICAL COUNCIL, Pastoral Constitution on the Church in the Modern World *Gaudium et Spes*, 15; Decree on the Church's Missionary Activity *Ad Gentes*, 22.

Reference to the sciences is often helpful, allowing as it does a more thorough knowledge of the subject under study; but it should not mean the rejection of a typically philosophical and critical thinking which is concerned with the universal. Indeed, this kind of thinking is required for a fruitful exchange between cultures. What I wish to emphasize is the duty to go beyond the particular and concrete, lest the prime task of demonstrating the universality of faith's content be abandoned. Nor should it be forgotten that the specific contribution of philosophical enquiry enables us to discern in different world-views and different cultures "not what people think but what the objective truth is".[93] It is not an array of human opinions but truth alone which can be of help to theology.

70. Because of its implications for both philosophy and theology, the question of the relationship with cultures calls for particular attention, which cannot however claim to be exhaustive. From the time the Gospel was first preached, the Church has known the process of encounter and engagement with cultures. Christ's mandate to his disciples to go out everywhere, "even to the ends of the earth" (*Acts* 1:8), in order to pass on the truth which he had revealed, led the Christian community to recognize from the first the universality of its message and the difficulties created

[93] SAINT THOMAS AQUINAS, *De Caelo*, 1, 22.

by cultural differences. A passage of Saint Paul's letter to the Christians of Ephesus helps us to understand how the early community responded to the problem. The Apostle writes: "Now in Christ Jesus you who once were far off have been brought near in the blood of Christ. For he is our peace, who has made us both one, and has broken down the wall of hostility" (2:13-14).

In the light of this text, we reflect further to see how the Gentiles were transformed once they had embraced the faith. With the richness of the salvation wrought by Christ, the walls separating the different cultures collapsed. God's promise in Christ now became a universal offer: no longer limited to one particular people, its language and its customs, but extended to all as a heritage from which each might freely draw. From their different locations and traditions all are called in Christ to share in the unity of the family of God's children. It is Christ who enables the two peoples to become "one". Those who were "far off" have come "near", thanks to the newness brought by the Paschal Mystery. Jesus destroys the walls of division and creates unity in a new and unsurpassed way through our sharing in his mystery. This unity is so deep that the Church can say with Saint Paul: "You are no longer strangers and sojourners, but you are saints and members of the household of God" (*Eph* 2:19).

This simple statement contains a great truth: faith's encounter with different cultures has created something new. When they are deeply rooted in experience, cultures show forth the human being's characteristic openness to the universal and the transcendent. Therefore they offer different paths to the truth, which assuredly serve men and women well in revealing values which can make their life ever more human.[94] Insofar as cultures appeal to the values of older traditions, they point—implicitly but authentically—to the manifestation of God in nature, as we saw earlier in considering the Wisdom literature and the teaching of Saint Paul.

71.   Inseparable as they are from people and their history, cultures share the dynamics which the human experience of life reveals. They change and advance because people meet in new ways and share with each other their ways of life. Cultures are fed by the communication of values, and they survive and flourish insofar as they remain open to assimilating new experiences. How are we to explain these dynamics? All people are part of a culture, depend upon it and shape it. Human beings are both child and parent of the culture in which they are immersed. To everything they do, they bring something which sets them apart from the rest of creation: their unfailing openness to mystery and their boundless desire for knowledge. Lying deep in every culture, there appears this impulse to-

[94] Cf. SECOND VATICAN ECUMENICAL COUNCIL, Pastoral Constitution on the Church in the Modern World *Gaudium et Spes*, 53-59.

wards a fulfilment. We may say, then, that culture itself has an intrinsic capacity to receive divine Revelation.

Cultural context permeates the living of Christian faith, which contributes in turn little by little to shaping that context. To every culture Christians bring the unchanging truth of God, which he reveals in the history and culture of a people. Time and again, therefore, in the course of the centuries we have seen repeated the event witnessed by the pilgrims in Jerusalem on the day of Pentecost. Hearing the Apostles, they asked one another: "Are not all these who are speaking Galileans? And how is it that we hear, each of us in his own native language? Parthians and Medes and Elamites and residents of Mesopotamia, Judea and Cappadocia, Pontus and Asia, Phrygia and Pamphylia, Egypt and the parts of Libya belonging to Cyrene, and visitors from Rome, both Jews and proselytes, Cretans and Arabians, we hear them telling in our own tongues the mighty works of God" (*Acts* 2:7-11). While it demands of all who hear it the adherence of faith, the proclamation of the Gospel in different cultures allows people to preserve their own cultural identity. This in no way creates division, because the community of the baptized is marked by a universality which can embrace every culture and help to foster whatever is implicit in them to the point where it will be fully explicit in the light of truth.

This means that no one culture can ever become the criterion of judgment, much less the ultimate criterion of truth with regard to God's Revelation. The Gospel is not opposed to any culture, as if in engaging a culture the Gospel would seek to strip it of its native riches and force it to adopt forms which are alien to it. On the contrary, the message which believers bring to the world and to cultures is a genuine liberation from all the disorders caused by sin and is, at the same time, a call to the fullness of truth. Cultures are not only not diminished by this encounter; rather, they are prompted to open themselves to the newness of the Gospel's truth and to be stirred by this truth to develop in new ways.

72.   In preaching the Gospel, Christianity first encountered Greek philosophy; but this does not mean at all that other approaches are precluded. Today, as the Gospel gradually comes into contact with cultural worlds which once lay beyond Christian influence, there are new tasks of inculturation, which mean that our generation faces problems not unlike those faced by the Church in the first centuries.

My thoughts turn immediately to the lands of the East, so rich in religious and philosophical traditions of great antiquity. Among these lands, India has a special place. A great spiritual impulse leads Indian thought to seek an experience which would liberate the spirit from the shackles of time and space and would therefore acquire absolute value. The dynamic of this quest for liberation provides the context for great metaphysical systems.

In India particularly, it is the duty of Christians now to draw from this rich heritage the elements compatible with their faith, in order to enrich Christian thought. In this work of discernment, which finds its inspiration in the Council's Declaration *Nostra Aetate*, certain criteria will have to be kept in mind. The first of these is the universality of the human spirit, whose basic needs are the same in the most disparate cultures. The second, which derives from the first, is this: in engaging great cultures for the first time, the Church cannot abandon what she has gained from her inculturation in the world of Greco-Latin thought. To reject this heritage would be to deny the providential plan of God who guides his Church down the paths of time and history. This criterion is valid for the Church in every age, even for the Church of the future, who will judge herself enriched by all that comes from today's engagement with Eastern cultures and will find in this inheritance fresh cues for fruitful dialogue with the cultures which will emerge as humanity moves into the future. Thirdly, care will need to be taken lest, contrary to the very nature of the human spirit, the legitimate defense of the uniqueness and originality of Indian thought be confused with the idea that a particular cultural tradition should remain closed in its difference and affirm itself by opposing other traditions.

What has been said here of India is no less true for the heritage of the great cultures of China, Japan and the other countries of Asia, as also for the riches of the traditional cultures of Africa, which are for the most part orally transmitted.

73. In the light of these considerations, the relationship between theology and philosophy is best construed as a circle. Theology's source and starting-point must always be the word of God revealed in history, while its final goal will be an understanding of that word which increases with each passing generation. Yet, since God's word is Truth (cf. *Jn* 17:17), the human search for truth—philosophy, pursued in keeping with its own rules—can only help to understand God's word better. It is not just a question of theological discourse using this or that concept or element of a philosophical construct; what matters most is that the believer's reason use its powers of reflection in the search for truth which moves from the word of God towards a better understanding of it. It is as if, moving between the twin poles of God's word and a better understanding of it, reason is offered guidance and is warned against paths which would lead it to stray from revealed Truth and to stray in the end from the truth pure and simple. Instead, reason is stirred to explore paths which of itself it would not even have suspected it could take.

This circular relationship with the word of God leaves philosophy enriched, because reason discovers new and unsuspected horizons.

74.   The fruitfulness of this relationship is confirmed by the experience of great Christian theologians who also distinguished themselves as great philosophers, bequeathing to us writings of such high speculative value as to warrant comparison with the masters of ancient philosophy. This is true of both the Fathers of the Church, among whom at least Saint Gregory of Nazianzus and Saint Augustine should be mentioned, and the Medieval Doctors with the great triad of Saint Anselm, Saint Bonaventure and Saint Thomas Aquinas. We see the same fruitful relationship between philosophy and the word of God in the courageous research pursued by more recent thinkers, among whom I gladly mention, in a Western context, figures such as John Henry Newman, Antonio Rosmini, Jacques Maritain, Étienne Gilson and Edith Stein and, in an Eastern context, eminent scholars such as Vladimir S. Soloviev, Pavel A. Florensky, Petr Chaadaev and Vladimir N. Lossky. Obviously other names could be cited; and in referring to these I intend not to endorse every aspect of their thought, but simply to offer significant examples of a process of philosophical enquiry which was enriched by engaging the data of faith. One thing is certain: attention to the spiritual journey of these masters can only give greater momentum to both the

search for truth and the effort to apply the results of that search to the service of humanity. It is to be hoped that now and in the future there will be those who continue to cultivate this great philosophical and theological tradition for the good of both the Church and humanity.

Different stances of philosophy

75. As appears from this brief sketch of the history of the relationship between faith and philosophy, one can distinguish different stances of philosophy with regard to Christian faith. First, there is a *philosophy completely independent of the Gospel's Revelation*: this is the stance adopted by philosophy as it took shape in history before the birth of the Redeemer and later in regions as yet untouched by the Gospel. We see here philosophy's valid aspiration to be an *autonomous* enterprise, obeying its own rules and employing the powers of reason alone. Although seriously handicapped by the inherent weakness of human reason, this aspiration should be supported and strengthened. As a search for truth within the natural order, the enterprise of philosophy is always open—at least implicitly—to the supernatural.

Moreover, the demand for a valid autonomy of thought should be respected even when theological discourse makes use of philosophical concepts and arguments. Indeed, to argue according to rigorous rational criteria is to guarantee that the results attained are universally valid. This also confirms the principle that grace does not destroy nature but perfects it: the assent of faith, engaging the intellect and will, does not destroy but perfects the free will of each believer who deep within welcomes what has been revealed.

It is clear that this legitimate approach is rejected by the theory of so-called "separate" philosophy, pursued by some modern philosophers. This theory claims for philosophy not only a valid autonomy, but a self-sufficiency of thought which is patently invalid. In refusing the truth offered by divine Revelation, philosophy only does itself damage, since this is to preclude access to a deeper knowledge of truth.

76.   A second stance adopted by philosophy is often designated as *Christian philosophy*. In itself, the term is valid, but it should not be misunderstood: it in no way intends to suggest that there is an official philosophy of the Church, since the faith as such is not a philosophy. The term seeks rather to indicate a Christian way of philosophizing, a philosophical speculation conceived in dynamic union with faith. It does not therefore refer simply to a philosophy developed by Christian philosophers who have striven in their research not to contradict the faith. The term Christian philosophy includes those important developments of philosophical thinking which would not have happened without the direct or indirect contribution of Christian faith.

Christian philosophy therefore has two aspects. The first is subjective, in the sense that faith purifies reason. As a theological virtue, faith liberates reason from presumption, the typical temptation of the philosopher. Saint Paul, the Fathers of the Church and, closer to our own time, philosophers such as Pascal and Kierkegaard reproached such presumption. The philosopher who learns humility will also find courage to tackle questions which are difficult to resolve if the data of Revelation are ignored—for example, the problem of evil and suffering, the personal nature of God and the question of the meaning of life or, more directly, the radical metaphysical question, "Why is there something rather than nothing?".

The second aspect of Christian philosophy is objective, in the sense that it concerns content. Revelation clearly proposes certain truths which might never have been discovered by reason unaided, although they are not of themselves inaccessible to reason. Among these truths is the notion of a free and personal God who is the Creator of the world, a truth which has been so crucial for the development of philosophical thinking, especially the philosophy of being. There is also the reality of sin, as it appears in the light of faith, which helps to shape an adequate philosophical formulation of the problem of evil. The notion of the person as a spiritual being is another of faith's specific contributions: the Christian proclamation of human dignity, equality and free-

111

dom has undoubtedly influenced modern philosophical thought. In more recent times, there has been the discovery that history as event—so central to Christian Revelation—is important for philosophy as well. It is no accident that this has become pivotal for a philosophy of history which stakes its claim as a new chapter in the human search for truth.

Among the objective elements of Christian philosophy we might also place the need to explore the rationality of certain truths expressed in Sacred Scripture, such as the possibility of man's supernatural vocation and original sin itself. These are tasks which challenge reason to recognize that there is something true and rational lying far beyond the straits within which it would normally be confined. These questions in fact broaden reason's scope for action.

In speculating on these questions, philosophers have not become theologians, since they have not sought to understand and expound the truths of faith on the basis of Revelation. They have continued working on their own terrain and with their own purely rational method, yet extending their research to new aspects of truth. It could be said that a good part of modern and contemporary philosophy would not exist without this stimulus of the word of God. This conclusion retains all its relevance, despite the disappointing fact that many thinkers in recent centuries have abandoned Christian orthodoxy.

77.   Philosophy presents another stance worth noting *when theology itself calls upon it*. Theology in fact has always needed and still needs philosophy's contribution. As a work of critical reason in the light of faith, theology presupposes and requires in all its research a reason formed and educated to concept and argument. Moreover, theology needs philosophy as a partner in dialogue in order to confirm the intelligibility and universal truth of its claims. It was not by accident that the Fathers of the Church and the Medieval theologians adopted non-Christian philosophies. This historical fact confirms the value of philosophy's *autonomy*, which remains unimpaired when theology calls upon it; but it shows as well the profound transformations which philosophy itself must undergo.

It was because of its noble and indispensable contribution that, from the Patristic period onwards, philosophy was called the *ancilla theologiae*. The title was not intended to indicate philosophy's servile submission or purely functional role with regard to theology. Rather, it was used in the sense in which Aristotle had spoken of the experimental sciences as "ancillary" to "*prima philosophia*". The term can scarcely be used today, given the principle of autonomy to which we have referred, but it has served throughout history to indicate the necessity of the link between the two sciences and the impossibility of their separation.

Were theologians to refuse the help of philosophy, they would run the risk of doing philosophy unwittingly and locking themselves within thought-structures poorly adapted to the understanding of faith. Were philosophers, for their part, to shun theology completely, they would be forced to master on their own the contents of Christian faith, as has been the case with some modern philosophers. Either way, the grounding principles of autonomy which every science rightly wants guaranteed would be seriously threatened.

When it adopts this stance, philosophy, like theology, comes more directly under the authority of the Magisterium and its discernment, because of the implications it has for the understanding of Revelation, as I have already explained. The truths of faith make certain demands which philosophy must respect whenever it engages theology.

78.   It should be clear in the light of these reflections why the Magisterium has repeatedly acclaimed the merits of Saint Thomas' thought and made him the guide and model for theological studies. This has not been in order to take a position on properly philosophical questions nor to demand adherence to particular theses. The Magisterium's intention has always been to show how Saint Thomas is an authentic model for all who seek the truth. In his thinking, the demands of reason and the power of faith found the most elevated synthesis ever attained by human thought, for he could defend the radical newness intro-

duced by Revelation without ever demeaning the venture proper to reason.

79.   Developing further what the Magisterium before me has taught, I intend in this final section to point out certain requirements which theology—and more fundamentally still, the word of God itself—makes today of philosophical thinking and contemporary philosophies. As I have already noted, philosophy must obey its own rules and be based upon its own principles; truth, however, can only be one. The content of Revelation can never debase the discoveries and legitimate autonomy of reason. Yet, conscious that it cannot set itself up as an absolute and exclusive value, reason on its part must never lose its capacity to question and to be questioned. By virtue of the splendour emanating from subsistent Being itself, revealed truth offers the fullness of light and will therefore illumine the path of philosophical enquiry. In short, Christian Revelation becomes the true point of encounter and engagement between philosophical and theological thinking in their reciprocal relationship. It is to be hoped therefore that theologians and philosophers will let themselves be guided by the authority of truth alone so that there will emerge a philosophy consonant with the word of God. Such a philosophy will be a place where Christian faith and human cultures may meet, a point of understanding between believer and non-believer. It will help lead believers to a stronger conviction that faith grows deeper

and more authentic when it is wedded to thought and does not reject it. It is again the Fathers who teach us this: "To believe is nothing other than to think with assent... Believers are also thinkers: in believing, they think and in thinking, they believe... If faith does not think, it is nothing".[95] And again: "If there is no assent, there is no faith, for without assent one does not really believe".[96]

[95] Saint Augustine, *De Praedestinatione Sanctorum*, 2, 5: *PL* 44, 963.

[96] Idem, *De Fide, Spe et Caritate*, 7: *CCL* 64, 61.

CHAPTER VII

CURRENT REQUIREMENTS
AND TASKS

The indispensable requirements of the word of God

80.   In Sacred Scripture are found elements, both implicit and explicit, which allow a vision of the human being and the world which has exceptional philosophical density. Christians have come to an ever deeper awareness of the wealth to be found in the sacred text. It is there that we learn that what we experience is not absolute: it is neither uncreated nor self-generating. God alone is the Absolute. From the Bible there emerges also a vision of man as *imago Dei*. This vision offers indications regarding man's life, his freedom and the immortality of the human spirit. Since the created world is not self-sufficient, every illusion of autonomy which would deny the essential dependence on God of every creature—the human being included—leads to dramatic situations which subvert the rational search for the harmony and the meaning of human life.

The problem of moral evil—the most tragic of evil's forms—is also addressed in the Bible, which tells us that such evil stems not from any material deficiency, but is a wound inflicted by the disordered exercise of human freedom. In the end, the word of God poses the problem of the meaning of life and proffers its response in directing the human being to Jesus Christ, the Incarnate Word of God, who is the perfect realization of human existence. A reading of the sacred text would reveal other aspects of this problem; but what emerges clearly is the rejection of all forms of relativism, materialism and pantheism.

The fundamental conviction of the "philosophy" found in the Bible is that the world and human life do have a meaning and look towards their fulfilment, which comes in Jesus Christ. The mystery of the Incarnation will always remain the central point of reference for an understanding of the enigma of human existence, the created world and God himself. The challenge of this mystery pushes philosophy to its limits, as reason is summoned to make its own a logic which brings down the walls within which it risks being confined. Yet only at this point does the meaning of life reach its defining moment. The intimate essence of God and of the human being become intelligible: in the mystery of the Incarnate Word, human nature and divine nature are safeguarded in all their autonomy, and at the same time the unique bond which sets them together in mutuality without confusion of any kind is revealed.[97]

---

[97] Cf. ECUMENICAL COUNCIL OF CHALCEDON, *Symbolum, Definitio*: DS 302.

81.   One of the most significant aspects of our current situation, it should be noted, is the "crisis of meaning". Perspectives on life and the world, often of a scientific temper, have so proliferated that we face an increasing fragmentation of knowledge. This makes the search for meaning difficult and often fruitless. Indeed, still more dramatically, in this maelstrom of data and facts in which we live and which seem to comprise the very fabric of life, many people wonder whether it still makes sense to ask about meaning. The array of theories which vie to give an answer, and the different ways of viewing and of interpreting the world and human life, serve only to aggravate this radical doubt, which can easily lead to scepticism, indifference or to various forms of nihilism.

In consequence, the human spirit is often invaded by a kind of ambiguous thinking which leads it to an ever deepening introversion, locked within the confines of its own immanence without reference of any kind to the transcendent. A philosophy which no longer asks the question of the meaning of life would be in grave danger of reducing reason to merely accessory functions, with no real passion for the search for truth.

To be consonant with the word of God, philosophy needs first of all to recover its *sapiential dimension* as a search for the ultimate and overarching meaning of life. This first requirement is in fact most helpful in stimulating philosophy to conform to its proper nature. In doing so, it will be not only the decisive critical factor which determines the foundations and limits of the different fields of scientific learning, but will also take its place as the ultimate framework of the unity of human knowledge and action, leading them to converge towards a final goal and meaning. This sapiential dimension is all the more necessary today, because the immense expansion of humanity's technical capability demands a renewed and sharpened sense of ultimate values. If this technology is not ordered to something greater than a merely utilitarian end, then it could soon prove inhuman and even become potential destroyer of the human race.[98]

The word of God reveals the final destiny of men and women and provides a unifying explanation of all that they do in the world. This is why it invites philosophy to engage in the search for the natural foundation of this meaning, which corresponds to the religious impulse innate in every person. A philosophy denying the possibility of an ultimate and overarching meaning would be not only ill-adapted to its task, but false.

82.   Yet this sapiential function could not be performed by a philosophy which was not itself a true and authentic knowledge, addressed, that is, not only to particular and subordinate aspects of reality—functional, formal or utilitarian—but to its total and definitive truth, to the very being of

[98] Cf. JOHN PAUL II, Encyclical Letter *Redemptor Hominis* (4 March 1979), 15: *AAS* 71 (1979), 286-289.

the object which is known. This prompts a second requirement: that philosophy verify the human capacity to *know the truth*, to come to a knowledge which can reach objective truth by means of that *adaequatio rei et intellectus* to which the Scholastic Doctors referred. [99] This requirement, proper to faith, was explicitly reaffirmed by the Second Vatican Council: "Intelligence is not confined to observable data alone. It can with genuine certitude attain to reality itself as knowable, though in consequence of sin that certitude is partially obscured and weakened". [100]

A radically phenomenalist or relativist philosophy would be ill-adapted to help in the deeper exploration of the riches found in the word of God. Sacred Scripture always assumes that the individual, even if guilty of duplicity and mendacity, can know and grasp the clear and simple truth. The Bible, and the New Testament in particular, contains texts and statements which have a genuinely ontological content. The inspired authors intended to formulate true statements, capable, that is, of expressing objective reality. It cannot be said that the Catholic tradition erred when it took certain texts of Saint John and Saint Paul to be statements about the very being of Christ. In seeking to understand and explain these statements, theology needs therefore the

[99] Cf., for example, SAINT THOMAS AQUINAS, *Summa Theologiae*, I, 16, 1; SAINT BONAVENTURE, *Coll. In Hex.*, 3, 8, 1.
[100] Pastoral Constitution on the Church in the Modern World *Gaudium et Spes*, 15.

contribution of a philosophy which does not disavow the possibility of a knowledge which is objectively true, even if not perfect. This applies equally to the judgements of moral conscience, which Sacred Scripture considers capable of being objectively true.[101]

83.   The two requirements already stipulated imply a third: the need for a philosophy of *genuinely metaphysical* range, capable, that is, of transcending empirical data in order to attain something absolute, ultimate and foundational in its search for truth. This requirement is implicit in sapiential and analytical knowledge alike; and in particular it is a requirement for knowing the moral good, which has its ultimate foundation in the Supreme Good, God himself. Here I do not mean to speak of metaphysics in the sense of a specific school or a particular historical current of thought. I want only to state that reality and truth do transcend the factual and the empirical, and to vindicate the human being's capacity to know this transcendent and metaphysical dimension in a way that is true and certain, albeit imperfect and analogical. In this sense, metaphysics should not be seen as an alternative to anthropology, since it is metaphysics which makes it possible to ground the concept of personal dignity in virtue of their spiritual nature. In a special way, the person constitutes a privileged locus for the

[101] Cf. JOHN PAUL II, Encyclical Letter *Veritatis Splendor* (6 August 1993), 57-61: *AAS* 85 (1993), 1179-1182.

encounter with being, and hence with metaphysical enquiry.

Wherever men and women discover a call to the absolute and transcendent, the metaphysical dimension of reality opens up before them: in truth, in beauty, in moral values, in other persons, in being itself, in God. We face a great challenge at the end of this millennium to move from *phenomenon* to *foundation*, a step as necessary as it is urgent. We cannot stop short at experience alone; even if experience does reveal the human being's interiority and spirituality, speculative thinking must penetrate to the spiritual core and the ground from which it rises. Therefore, a philosophy which shuns metaphysics would be radically unsuited to the task of mediation in the understanding of Revelation.

The word of God refers constantly to things which transcend human experience and even human thought; but this "mystery" could not be revealed, nor could theology render it in some way intelligible,[102] were human knowledge limited strictly to the world of sense experience. Metaphysics thus plays an essential role of mediation in theological research. A theology without a metaphysical horizon could not move beyond an analysis of religious experience, nor would it allow the *intellectus fidei* to give a coherent account of the universal and transcendent value of revealed truth.

---

[102] Cf. FIRST VATICAN ECUMENICAL COUNCIL, Dogmatic Constitution on the Catholic Faith *Dei Filius*, IV: *DS* 3016.

If I insist so strongly on the metaphysical element, it is because I am convinced that it is the path to be taken in order to move beyond the crisis pervading large sectors of philosophy at the moment, and thus to correct certain mistaken modes of behaviour now widespread in our society.

84.   The importance of metaphysics becomes still more evident if we consider current developments in hermeneutics and the analysis of language. The results of such studies can be very helpful for the understanding of faith, since they bring to light the structure of our thought and speech and the meaning which language bears. However, some scholars working in these fields tend to stop short at the question of how reality is understood and expressed, without going further to see whether reason can discover its essence. How can we fail to see in such a frame of mind the confirmation of our present crisis of confidence in the powers of reason? When, on the basis of preconceived assumptions, these positions tend to obscure the contents of faith or to deny their universal validity, then not only do they abase reason but in so doing they also disqualify themselves. Faith clearly presupposes that human language is capable of expressing divine and transcendent reality in a universal way—analogically, it is true, but no less mean-

ingfully for that.[103] Were this not so, the word of God, which is always a divine word in human language, would not be capable of saying anything about God. The interpretation of this word cannot merely keep referring us to one interpretation after another, without ever leading us to a statement which is simply true; otherwise there would be no Revelation of God, but only the expression of human notions about God and about what God presumably thinks of us.

85. I am well aware that these requirements which the word of God imposes upon philosophy may seem daunting to many people involved in philosophical research today. Yet this is why, taking up what has been taught repeatedly by the Popes for several generations and reaffirmed by the Second Vatican Council itself, I wish to reaffirm strongly the conviction that the human being can come to a unified and organic vision of knowledge. This is one of the tasks which Christian thought will have to take up through the next millennium of the Christian era. The segmentation of knowledge, with its splintered approach to truth and consequent fragmentation of meaning, keeps people today from coming to an interior unity. How could the Church not be concerned by this? It is the Gospel which imposes this sapiential task directly upon her Pastors,

[103] Cf. FOURTH LATERAN ECUMENICAL COUNCIL, *De Errore Abbatis Ioachim*, II: *DS* 806.

and they cannot shrink from their duty to undertake it.

I believe that those philosophers who wish to respond today to the demands which the word of God makes on human thinking should develop their thought on the basis of these postulates and in organic continuity with the great tradition which, beginning with the ancients, passes through the Fathers of the Church and the masters of Scholasticism and includes the fundamental achievements of modern and contemporary thought. If philosophers can take their place within this tradition and draw their inspiration from it, they will certainly not fail to respect philosophy's demand for autonomy.

In the present situation, therefore, it is most significant that some philosophers are promoting a recovery of the determining role of this tradition for a right approach to knowledge. The appeal to tradition is not a mere remembrance of the past; it involves rather the recognition of a cultural heritage which belongs to all of humanity. Indeed it may be said that it is we who belong to the tradition and that it is not ours to dispose of at will. Precisely by being rooted in the tradition will we be able today to develop for the future an original, new and constructive mode of thinking. This same appeal is all the more valid for theology. Not only because theology has the living Tradition of the Church as its original source,[104] but also because, in virtue of this, it must be able to recover both the profound theological tradition of earlier times and the enduring tradition of that philosophy which by dint of its authentic wisdom can transcend the boundaries of space and time.

86.   This insistence on the need for a close relationship of continuity between contemporary philosophy and the philosophy developed in the Christian tradition is intended to avert the danger which lies hidden in some currents of thought which are especially prevalent today. It is appropriate, I think, to review them, however briefly, in order to point out their errors and the consequent risks for philosophical work.

The first goes by the name of *eclecticism*, by which is meant the approach of those who, in research, teaching and argumentation, even in theology, tend to use individual ideas drawn from different philosophies, without concern for their internal coherence, their place within a system or their historical context. They therefore run the risk of being unable to distinguish the part of truth of a given doctrine from elements of it which may be erroneous or ill-suited to the task at hand. An extreme form of eclecticism appears also in the rhetorical misuse of philosophical terms to which some theologians are given at

[104] Cf. SECOND VATICAN ECUMENICAL COUNCIL, Dogmatic Constitution on Divine Revelation *Dei Verbum*, 24; Decree on Priestly Formation *Optatam Totius*, 16.

times. Such manipulation does not help the search for truth and does not train reason—whether theological or philosophical—to formulate arguments seriously and scientifically. The rigorous and far-reaching study of philosophical doctrines, their particular terminology and the context in which they arose, helps to overcome the danger of eclecticism and makes it possible to integrate them into theological discourse in a way appropriate to the task.

87.   Eclecticism is an error of method, but lying hidden within it can also be the claims of *historicism*. To understand a doctrine from the past correctly, it is necessary to set it within its proper historical and cultural context. The fundamental claim of historicism, however, is that the truth of a philosophy is determined on the basis of its appropriateness to a certain period and a certain historical purpose. At least implicitly, therefore, the enduring validity of truth is denied. What was true in one period, historicists claim, may not be true in another. Thus for them the history of thought becomes little more than an archeological resource useful for illustrating positions once held, but for the most part outmoded and meaningless now. On the contrary, it should not be forgotten that, even if a formulation is bound in some way by time and culture, the truth or the error which it expresses can invariably be identified and evaluated as such despite the distance of space and time.

In theological enquiry, historicism tends to appear for the most part under the guise of "modernism". Rightly concerned to make theological discourse relevant and understandable to our time, some theologians use only the most recent opinions and philosophical language, ignoring the critical evaluation which ought to be made of them in the light of the tradition. By exchanging relevance for truth, this form of modernism shows itself incapable of satisfying the demands of truth to which theology is called to respond.

88. Another threat to be reckoned with is *scientism*. This is the philosophical notion which refuses to admit the validity of forms of knowledge other than those of the positive sciences; and it relegates religious, theological, ethical and aesthetic knowledge to the realm of mere fantasy. In the past, the same idea emerged in positivism and neo-positivism, which considered metaphysical statements to be meaningless. Critical epistemology has discredited such a claim, but now we see it revived in the new guise of scientism, which dismisses values as mere products of the emotions and rejects the notion of being in order to clear the way for pure and simple facticity. Science would thus be poised to dominate all aspects of human life through technological progress. The undeniable triumphs of scientific research and contemporary technology have helped to propagate a scientistic outlook, which

now seems boundless, given its inroads into different cultures and the radical changes it has brought.

Regrettably, it must be noted, scientism consigns all that has to do with the question of the meaning of life to the realm of the irrational or imaginary. No less disappointing is the way in which it approaches the other great problems of philosophy which, if they are not ignored, are subjected to analyses based on superficial analogies, lacking all rational foundation. This leads to the impoverishment of human thought, which no longer addresses the ultimate problems which the human being, as the *animal rationale*, has pondered constantly from the beginning of time. And since it leaves no space for the critique offered by ethical judgement, the scientistic mentality has succeeded in leading many to think that if something is technically possible it is therefore morally admissible.

89. No less dangerous is *pragmatism*, an attitude of mind which, in making its choices, precludes theoretical considerations or judgements based on ethical principles. The practical consequences of this mode of thinking are significant. In particular there is growing support for a concept of democracy which is not grounded upon any reference to unchanging values: whether or not a line of action is admissible is decided by

the vote of a parliamentary majority.[105] The consequences of this are clear: in practice, the great moral decisions of humanity are subordinated to decisions taken one after another by institutional agencies. Moreover, anthropology itself is severely compromised by a one-dimensional vision of the human being, a vision which excludes the great ethical dilemmas and the existential analyses of the meaning of suffering and sacrifice, of life and death.

90.   The positions we have examined lead in turn to a more general conception which appears today as the common framework of many philosophies which have rejected the meaningfulness of being. I am referring to the nihilist interpretation, which is at once the denial of all foundations and the negation of all objective truth. Quite apart from the fact that it conflicts with the demands and the content of the word of God, *nihilism* is a denial of the humanity and of the very identity of the human being. It should never be forgotten that the neglect of being inevitably leads to losing touch with objective truth and therefore with the very ground of human dignity. This in turn makes it possible to erase from the countenance of man and woman the marks of their likeness to God, and thus to lead them little by little either to a destructive will to power or to a solitude without hope. Once the

[105] Cf. JOHN PAUL II, Encyclical Letter *Evangelium Vitae* (25 March 1995), 69: *AAS* 87 (1995), 481.

truth is denied to human beings, it is pure illusion to try to set them free. Truth and freedom either go together hand in hand or together they perish in misery.[106]

91.   In discussing these currents of thought, it has not been my intention to present a complete picture of the present state of philosophy, which would, in any case, be difficult to reduce to a unified vision. And I certainly wish to stress that our heritage of knowledge and wisdom has indeed been enriched in different fields. We need only cite logic, the philosophy of language, epistemology, the philosophy of nature, anthropology, the more penetrating analysis of the affective dimensions of knowledge and the existential approach to the analysis of freedom. Since the last century, however, the affirmation of the principle of immanence, central to the rationalist argument, has provoked a radical requestioning of claims once thought indisputable. In response, currents

---

[106] In the same sense I commented in my first Encyclical Letter on the expression in the Gospel of Saint John, "You will know the truth, and the truth will set you free" (8:32): "These words contain both a fundamental requirement and a warning: the requirement of an honest relationship with regard to truth as a condition for authentic freedom, and the warning to avoid every kind of illusory freedom, every superficial unilateral freedom, every freedom that fails to enter into the whole truth about man and the world. Today also, even after two thousand years, we see Christ as the one who brings man freedom based on truth, frees man from what curtails, diminishes and as it were breaks off this freedom at its root, in man's soul, his heart and his conscience": Encyclical Letter *Redemptor Hominis* (4 March 1979), 12: *AAS* 71 (1979), 280-281.

of irrationalism arose, even as the baselessness of the demand that reason be absolutely self-grounded was being critically demonstrated.

Our age has been termed by some thinkers the age of "postmodernity". Often used in very different contexts, the term designates the emergence of a complex of new factors which, widespread and powerful as they are, have shown themselves able to produce important and lasting changes. The term was first used with reference to aesthetic, social and technological phenomena. It was then transposed into the philosophical field, but has remained somewhat ambiguous, both because judgement on what is called "postmodern" is sometimes positive and sometimes negative, and because there is as yet no consensus on the delicate question of the demarcation of the different historical periods. One thing however is certain: the currents of thought which claim to be postmodern merit appropriate attention. According to some of them, the time of certainties is irrevocably past, and the human being must now learn to live in a horizon of total absence of meaning, where everything is provisional and ephemeral. In their destructive critique of every certitude, several authors have failed to make crucial distinctions and have called into question the certitudes of faith.

This nihilism has been justified in a sense by the terrible experience of evil which has marked our age. Such a dramatic experience has ensured the collapse of rationalist optimism, which viewed history as the triumphant progress of reason, the source of all happiness and freedom; and now, at the end of this century, one of our greatest threats is the temptation to despair.

Even so, it remains true that a certain positivist cast of mind continues to nurture the illusion that, thanks to scientific and technical progress, man and woman may live as a demiurge, single-handedly and completely taking charge of their destiny.

Current tasks for theology

92.   As an understanding of Revelation, theology has always had to respond in different historical moments to the demands of different cultures, in order then to mediate the content of faith to those cultures in a coherent and conceptually clear way. Today, too, theology faces a dual task. On the one hand, it must be increasingly committed to the task entrusted to it by the Second Vatican Council, the task of renewing its specific methods in order to serve evangelization more effectively. How can we fail to recall in this regard the words of Pope John XXIII at the opening of the Council? He said then: "In line with the keen expectation of those who sincerely love the Christian, Catholic and apostolic religion, this doctrine must be known more widely and deeply, and souls must be instructed and formed in it more completely; and this certain and unchangeable doctrine, always to be faithfully respected,

must be understood more profoundly and presented in a way which meets the needs of our time".[107]

On the other hand, theology must look to the ultimate truth which Revelation entrusts to it, never content to stop short of that goal. Theologians should remember that their work corresponds "to a dynamism found in the faith itself" and that the proper object of their enquiry is "the Truth which is the living God and his plan for salvation revealed in Jesus Christ".[108] This task, which is theology's prime concern, challenges philosophy as well. The array of problems which today need to be tackled demands a joint effort—approached, it is true, with different methods—so that the truth may once again be known and expressed. The Truth, which is Christ, imposes itself as an all-embracing authority which holds out to theology and philosophy alike the prospect of support, stimulation and increase (cf. *Eph* 4:15).

To believe it possible to know a universally valid truth is in no way to encourage intolerance; on the contrary, it is the essential condition for sincere and authentic dialogue between persons. On this basis alone is it possible to overcome divisions and to journey together towards full truth,

[107] Address at the Opening of the Council (11 October 1962): *AAS* 54 (1962), 792.

[108] CONGREGATION FOR THE DOCTRINE OF THE FAITH, Instruction on the Ecclesial Vocation of the Theologian *Donum Veritatis* (24 May 1990), 7-8: *AAS* 82 (1990), 1552-1553.

walking those paths known only to the Spirit of the Risen Lord.[109] I wish at this point to indicate the specific form which the call to unity now takes, given the current tasks of theology.

93. The chief purpose of theology is to *provide an understanding of Revelation and the content of faith*. The very heart of theological enquiry will thus be the contemplation of the mystery of the Triune God. The approach to this mystery begins with reflection upon the mystery of the Incarnation of the Son of God: his coming as man, his going to his Passion and Death, a mystery issuing into his glorious Resurrection and Ascension to the right hand of the Father, whence he would send the Spirit of truth to bring his Church to birth and give her growth. From this vantage-point, the prime commitment of theology is seen to be the understanding of God's *kenosis*,

---

[109] In the Encyclical Letter *Dominum et Vivificantem*, commenting on *Jn* 16:12-13, I wrote: "Jesus presents the Comforter, the Spirit of truth, as the one who 'will teach' and 'bring to remembrance', as the one who 'will bear witness' to him. Now he says: 'he will guide you into all the truth'. This 'guiding into all the truth', referring to what the Apostles 'cannot bear now', is necessarily connected with Christ's self-emptying through his Passion and Death on the Cross, which, when he spoke these words, was just about to happen. Later however it becomes clear that this 'guiding into all the truth' is connected not only with the *scandalum Crucis*, but also with everything that Christ 'did and taught' (*Acts* 1:1). For the *mysterium Christi* taken as a whole demands faith, since it is faith that adequately introduces man into the reality of the revealed mystery. The 'guiding into all the truth' is therefore achieved in faith and through faith: and this is the work of the Spirit of truth and the result of his action in man. Here the Holy Spirit is to be man's supreme guide and the light of the human spirit": No. 6: *AAS* 78 (1986), 815-816.

a grand and mysterious truth for the human mind, which finds it inconceivable that suffering and death can express a love which gives itself and seeks nothing in return. In this light, a careful analysis of texts emerges as a basic and urgent need: first the texts of Scripture, and then those which express the Church's living Tradition. On this score, some problems have emerged in recent times, problems which are only partially new; and a coherent solution to them will not be found without philosophy's contribution.

94.   An initial problem is that of the relationship between meaning and truth. Like every other text, the sources which the theologian interprets primarily transmit a meaning which needs to be grasped and explained. This meaning presents itself as the truth about God which God himself communicates through the sacred text. Human language thus embodies the language of God, who communicates his own truth with that wonderful "condescension" which mirrors the logic of the Incarnation.[110] In interpreting the sources of Revelation, then, the theologian needs to ask what is the deep and authentic truth which the texts wish to communicate, even within the limits of language.

The truth of the biblical texts, and of the Gospels in particular, is certainly not restricted to the narration of simple historical events or the

[110] Cf. SECOND VATICAN ECUMENICAL COUNCIL, Dogmatic Constitution on Divine Revelation *Dei Verbum*, 13.

statement of neutral facts, as historicist positivism would claim.[111] Beyond simple historical occurrence, the truth of the events which these texts relate lies rather in the meaning they have *in* and *for* the history of salvation. This truth is elaborated fully in the Church's constant reading of these texts over the centuries, a reading which preserves intact their original meaning. There is a pressing need, therefore, that the relationship between fact and meaning, a relationship which constitutes the specific sense of history, be examined also from the philosophical point of view.

95.   The word of God is not addressed to any one people or to any one period of history. Similarly, dogmatic statements, while reflecting at times the culture of the period in which they were defined, formulate an unchanging and ultimate truth. This prompts the question of how one can reconcile the absoluteness and the universality of truth with the unavoidable historical and cultural conditioning of the formulas which express that truth. The claims of historicism, I noted earlier, are untenable; but the use of a hermeneutic open to the appeal of metaphysics can show how it is possible to move from the historical and contingent circumstances in which the texts developed to the truth which they express, a truth transcending those circumstances.

[111] Cf. PONTIFICAL BIBLICAL COMMISSION, Instruction on the Historical Truth of the Gospels (21 April 1964): *AAS* 56 (1964), 713.

Human language may be conditioned by history and constricted in other ways, but the human being can still express truths which surpass the phenomenon of language. Truth can never be confined to time and culture; in history it is known, but it also reaches beyond history.

96.   To see this is to glimpse the solution of another problem: the problem of the enduring validity of the conceptual language used in Conciliar definitions. This is a question which my revered predecessor Pius XII addressed in his Encyclical Letter *Humani Generis*.[112]

This is a complex theme to ponder, since one must reckon seriously with the meaning which words assume in different times and cultures. Nonetheless, the history of thought shows that across the range of cultures and their development certain basic concepts retain their universal epistemological value and thus retain the truth

---

[112] "It is clear that the Church cannot be tied to any and every passing philosophical system. Nevertheless, those notions and terms which have been developed though common effort by Catholic teachers over the course of the centuries to bring about some understanding of dogma are certainly not based on any such weak foundation. They are based on principles and notions deduced from a true knowledge of created things. In the process of deduction, this knowledge, like a star, gave enlightenment to the human mind through the Church. Hence it is not astonishing that some of these notions have not only been employed by the Ecumenical Councils, but even sanctioned by them, so that it is wrong to depart from them": Encyclical Letter *Humani Generis* (12 August 1950): *AAS* 42 (1950), 566-567; cf. INTERNATIONAL THEOLOGICAL COMMISSION, Document *Interpretationis Problema* (October 1989): *Enchiridion Vaticanum* 11, 2717-2811.

of the propositions in which they are expressed.[113] Were this not the case, philosophy and the sciences could not communicate with each other, nor could they find a place in cultures different from those in which they were conceived and developed. The hermeneutical problem exists, to be sure; but it is not insoluble. Moreover, the objective value of many concepts does not exclude that their meaning is often imperfect. This is where philosophical speculation can be very helpful. We may hope, then, that philosophy will be especially concerned to deepen the understanding of the relationship between conceptual language and truth, and to propose ways which will lead to a right understanding of that relationship.

97.   The interpretation of sources is a vital task for theology; but another still more delicate and demanding task is the *understanding of revealed truth*, or the articulation of the *intellectus fidei*. The *intellectus fidei*, as I have noted, demands the contribution of a philosophy of being which first of all would enable *dogmatic theology* to perform its functions appropriately. The dogmatic pragma-

[113] "As for the meaning of dogmatic formulas, this remains ever true and constant in the Church, even when it is expressed with greater clarity or more developed. The faithful therefore must shun the opinion, first, that dogmatic formulas (or some category of them) cannot signify the truth in a determinate way, but can only offer changeable approximations to it, which to a certain extent distort or alter it": SACRED CONGREGATION FOR THE DOCTRINE OF THE FAITH, Declaration in Defence of the Catholic Doctrine on the Church *Mysterium Ecclesiae* (24 June 1973), 5: *AAS* 65 (1973), 403.

tism of the early years of this century, which viewed the truths of faith as nothing more than rules of conduct, has already been refuted and rejected; [114] but the temptation always remains of understanding these truths in purely functional terms. This leads only to an approach which is inadequate, reductive and superficial at the level of speculation. A Christology, for example, which proceeded solely "from below", as is said nowadays, or an ecclesiology developed solely on the model of civil society, would be hard pressed to avoid the danger of such reductionism.

If the *intellectus fidei* wishes to integrate all the wealth of the theological tradition, it must turn to the philosophy of being, which should be able to propose anew the problem of being—and this in harmony with the demands and insights of the entire philosophical tradition, including philosophy of more recent times, without lapsing into sterile repetition of antiquated formulas. Set within the Christian metaphysical tradition, the philosophy of being is a dynamic philosophy which views reality in its ontological, causal and communicative structures. It is strong and enduring because it is based upon the very act of being itself, which allows a full and comprehensive openness to reality as a whole, surpassing every limit in order to reach the One who brings all

[114] Cf. CONGREGATION OF THE HOLY OFFICE, Decree *Lamentabili* (3 July 1907), 26: *ASS* 40 (1907), 473.

things to fulfilment.[115] In theology, which draws its principles from Revelation as a new source of knowledge, this perspective is confirmed by the intimate relationship which exists between faith and metaphysical reasoning.

98. These considerations apply equally to *moral theology*. It is no less urgent that philosophy be recovered at the point where the understanding of faith is linked to the moral life of believers. Faced with contemporary challenges in the social, economic, political and scientific fields, the ethical conscience of people is disoriented. In the Encyclical Letter *Veritatis Splendor*, I wrote that many of the problems of the contemporary world stem from a crisis of truth. I noted that "once the idea of a universal truth about the good, knowable by human reason, is lost, inevitably the notion of conscience also changes. Conscience is no longer considered in its prime reality as an act of a person's intelligence, the function of which is to apply the universal knowledge of the good in a specific situation and thus to express a judgment about the right conduct to be chosen here and now. Instead, there is a tendency to grant to the individual conscience the prerogative of independently determining the criteria of good and evil and then acting accordingly. Such an outlook is quite congenial to an individualist eth-

[115] Cf. JOHN PAUL II, Address to the Pontifical Athenaeum "Angelicum" (17 November 1979), 6: *Insegnamenti,* II, 2 (1979), 1183-1185.

ic, wherein each individual is faced with his own truth different from the truth of others".[116]

Throughout the Encyclical I underscored clearly the fundamental role of truth in the moral field. In the case of the more pressing ethical problems, this truth demands of moral theology a careful enquiry rooted unambiguously in the word of God. In order to fulfil its mission, moral theology must turn to a philosophical ethics which looks to the truth of the good, to an ethics which is neither subjectivist nor utilitarian. Such an ethics implies and presupposes a philosophical anthropology and a metaphysics of the good. Drawing on this organic vision, linked necessarily to Christian holiness and to the practice of the human and supernatural virtues, moral theology will be able to tackle the various problems in its competence, such as peace, social justice, the family, the defence of life and the natural environment, in a more appropriate and effective way.

99.   Theological work in the Church is first of all at the service of the proclamation of the faith and of catechesis.[117] Proclamation or kerygma is a call to conversion, announcing the truth of Christ, which reaches its summit in his Paschal Mystery: for only in Christ is it possible to know the full-

---

[116] No. 32: *AAS* 85 (1993), 1159-1160.

[117] Cf. JOHN PAUL II, Apostolic Exhortation *Catechesi Tradendae* (16 October 1979), 30: *AAS* 71 (1979), 1302-1303; CONGREGATION FOR THE DOCTRINE OF THE FAITH, Instruction on the Ecclesial Vocation of the Theologian *Donum Veritatis* (24 May 1990), 7: *AAS* 82 (1990), 1552-1553.

ness of the truth which saves (cf. *Acts* 4:12; 1 *Tm* 2:4-6).

In this respect, it is easy to see why, in addition to theology, reference to *catechesis* is also important, since catechesis has philosophical implications which must be explored more deeply in the light of faith. The teaching imparted in catechesis helps to form the person. As a mode of linguistic communication, catechesis must present the Church's doctrine in its integrity,[118] demonstrating its link with the life of the faithful.[119] The result is a unique bond between teaching and living which is otherwise unattainable, since what is communicated in catechesis is not a body of conceptual truths, but the mystery of the living God.[120]

Philosophical enquiry can help greatly to clarify the relationship between truth and life, between event and doctrinal truth, and above all between transcendent truth and humanly comprehensible language.[121] This involves a reciprocity between the theological disciplines and the insights drawn from the various strands of philosophy; and such a reciprocity can prove genuinely fruitful for the communication and deeper understanding of the faith.

---

[118] Cf. JOHN PAUL II, Apostolic Exhortation *Catechesi Tradendae* (16 October 1979), 30: *AAS* 71 (1979), 1302-1303.

[119] Cf. *ibid.*, 22, *loc. cit.*, 1295-1296.

[120] Cf. *ibid.*, 7, *loc. cit.*, 1282.

[121] Cf. *ibid.*, 59, *loc. cit.*, 1325.

CONCLUSION

100.   More than a hundred years after the appearance of Pope Leo XIII's Encyclical *Aeterni Patris*, to which I have often referred in these pages, I have sensed the need to revisit in a more systematic way the issue of the relationship between faith and philosophy. The importance of philosophical thought in the development of culture and its influence on patterns of personal and social behaviour is there for all to see. In addition, philosophy exercises a powerful, though not always obvious, influence on theology and its disciplines. For these reasons, I have judged it appropriate and necessary to emphasize the value of philosophy for the understanding of the faith, as well as the limits which philosophy faces when it neglects or rejects the truths of Revelation. The Church remains profoundly convinced that faith and reason "mutually support each other"; [122] each influences the other, as they offer to each other a purifying critique and a stimulus to pursue the search for deeper understanding.

---

[122] FIRST VATICAN ECUMENICAL COUNCIL, Dogmatic Constitution on the Catholic Faith *Dei Filius*, IV: *DS* 3019.

101.   A survey of the history of thought, especially in the West, shows clearly that the encounter between philosophy and theology and the
exchange of their respective insights have con-
tributed richly to the progress of humanity. Endowed as it is with an openness and originality
which allow it to stand as the science of faith,
theology has certainly challenged reason to remain
open to the radical newness found in God's Revelation; and this has been an undoubted boon for
philosophy which has thus glimpsed new vistas of
further meanings which reason is summoned to
penetrate.

Precisely in the light of this consideration,
and just as I have reaffirmed theology's duty to
recover its true relationship with philosophy, I
feel equally bound to stress how right it is that,
for the benefit and development of human
thought, philosophy too should recover its relationship with theology. In theology, philosophy
will find not the thinking of a single person
which, however rich and profound, still entails
the limited perspective of an individual, but the
wealth of a communal reflection. For by its very
nature, theology is sustained in the search for
truth by its *ecclesial context* [123] and by the tradition
of the People of God, with its harmony of many

[123] "Nobody can make of theology as it were a simple col-
lection of his own personal ideas, but everybody must be aware
of being in close union with the mission of teaching truth for
which the Church is responsible": JOHN PAUL II, Encyclical
Letter *Redemptor Hominis* (4 March 1979), 19: *AAS* 71 (1979), 308.

different fields of learning and culture within the unity of faith.

102. Insisting on the importance and true range of philosophical thought, the Church promotes both the defence of human dignity and the proclamation of the Gospel message. There is today no more urgent preparation for the performance of these tasks than this: to lead people to discover both their capacity to know the truth [124] and their yearning for the ultimate and definitive meaning of life. In the light of these profound needs, inscribed by God in human nature, the human and humanizing meaning of God's word also emerges more clearly. Through the mediation of a philosophy which is also true wisdom, people today will come to realize that their humanity is all the more affirmed the more they entrust themselves to the Gospel and open themselves to Christ.

103. Philosophy moreover is the mirror which reflects the culture of a people. A philosophy which responds to the challenge of theology's demands and evolves in harmony with faith is part of that "evangelization of culture" which Paul VI proposed as one of the fundamental goals of evangelization.[125] I have unstintingly recalled the

---

[124] Cf. SECOND VATICAN ECUMENICAL COUNCIL, Declaration on Religious Freedom *Dignitatis Humanae*, 1-3.
[125] Cf. Apostolic Exhortation *Evangelii Nuntiandi* (8 December 1975), 20: *AAS* 68 (1976), 18-19.

pressing need for a *new evangelization*; and I appeal now to philosophers to explore more comprehensively the dimensions of the true, the good and the beautiful to which the word of God gives access. This task becomes all the more urgent if we consider the challenges which the new millennium seems to entail, and which affect in a particular way regions and cultures which have a long-standing Christian tradition. This attention to philosophy too should be seen as a fundamental and original contribution in service of the new evangelization.

104. Philosophical thought is often the only ground for understanding and dialogue with those who do not share our faith. The current ferment in philosophy demands of believing philosophers an attentive and competent commitment, able to discern the expectations, the points of openness and the key issues of this historical moment. Reflecting in the light of reason and in keeping with its rules, and guided always by the deeper understanding given them by the word of God, Christian philosophers can develop a reflection which will be both comprehensible and appealing to those who do not yet grasp the full truth which divine Revelation declares. Such a ground for understanding and dialogue is all the more vital nowadays, since the most pressing issues facing humanity—ecology, peace and the co-existence of different races and cultures, for instance—may possibly find a solution if there is a

clear and honest collaboration between Christians and the followers of other religions and all those who, while not sharing a religious belief, have at heart the renewal of humanity. The Second Vatican Council said as much: "For our part, the desire for such dialogue, undertaken solely out of love for the truth and with all due prudence, excludes no one, neither those who cultivate the values of the human spirit while not yet acknowledging their Source, nor those who are hostile to the Church and persecute her in various ways".[126] A philosophy in which there shines even a glimmer of the truth of Christ, the one definitive answer to humanity's problems,[127] will provide a potent underpinning for the true and planetary ethics which the world now needs.

105. In concluding this Encyclical Letter, my thoughts turn particularly to *theologians*, encouraging them to pay special attention to the philosophical implications of the word of God and to be sure to reflect in their work all the speculative and practical breadth of the science of theology. I wish to thank them for their service to the Church. The intimate bond between theological and philosophical wisdom is one of the Christian tradition's most distinctive treasures in the exploration of revealed truth. This is why I urge them to recover and express to the full the metaphysi-

---

[126] Pastoral Constitution on the Church in the Modern World *Gaudium et Spes*, 92.
[127] Cf. *ibid.*, 10.

cal dimension of truth in order to enter into a demanding critical dialogue with both contemporary philosophical thought and with the philosophical tradition in all its aspects, whether consonant with the word of God or not. Let theologians always remember the words of that great master of thought and spirituality, Saint Bonaventure, who in introducing his *Itinerarium Mentis in Deum* invites the reader to recognize the inadequacy of "reading without repentance, knowledge without devotion, research without the impulse of wonder, prudence without the ability to surrender to joy, action divorced from religion, learning sundered from love, intelligence without humility, study unsustained by divine grace, thought without the wisdom inspired by God".[128]

I am thinking too of those *responsible for priestly formation*, whether academic or pastoral. I encourage them to pay special attention to the philosophical preparation of those who will proclaim the Gospel to the men and women of today and, even more, of those who will devote themselves to theological research and teaching. They must make every effort to carry out their work in the light of the directives laid down by the Second Vatican Council [129] and subsequent legislation, which speak clearly of the urgent and binding obligation, incumbent on all, to contribute to a genuine and profound communica-

---

[128] *Prologus*, 4: *Opera Omnia*, Florence, 1891, vol. V, 296.
[129] Cf. Decree on Priestly Formation *Optatam Totius*, 15.

tion of the truths of the faith. The grave responsibility to provide for the appropriate training of those charged with teaching philosophy both in seminaries and ecclesiastical faculties must not be neglected.[130] Teaching in this field necessarily entails a suitable scholarly preparation, a systematic presentation of the great heritage of the Christian tradition and due discernment in the light of the current needs of the Church and the world.

106.   I appeal also to *philosophers*, and to all *teachers of philosophy*, asking them to have the courage to recover, in the flow of an enduringly valid philosophical tradition, the range of authentic wisdom and truth—metaphysical truth included—which is proper to philosophical enquiry. They should be open to the impelling questions which arise from the word of God and they should be strong enough to shape their thought and discussion in response to that challenge. Let them always strive for truth, alert to the good which truth contains. Then they will be able to formulate the genuine ethics which humanity needs so urgently at this particular time. The Church follows the work of philosophers with interest and appreciation; and they should rest assured of her respect for the rightful autonomy of their discipline. I would want especially to encourage believers working in the philosophical field to illumine the range of human activity by

[130] Cf. JOHN PAUL II, Apostolic Constitution *Sapientia Christiana* (15 April 1979), Arts. 67-68: *AAS* 71 (1979), 491-492.

the exercise of a reason which grows more penetrating and assured because of the support it receives from faith.

Finally, I cannot fail to address a word to *scientists*, whose research offers an ever greater knowledge of the universe as a whole and of the incredibly rich array of its component parts, animate and inanimate, with their complex atomic and molecular structures. So far has science come, especially in this century, that its achievements never cease to amaze us. In expressing my admiration and in offering encouragement to these brave pioneers of scientific research, to whom humanity owes so much of its current development, I would urge them to continue their efforts without ever abandoning the *sapiential* horizon within which scientific and technological achievements are wedded to the philosophical and ethical values which are the distinctive and indelible mark of the human person. Scientists are well aware that "the search for truth, even when it concerns a finite reality of the world or of man, is never-ending, but always points beyond to something higher than the immediate object of study, to the questions which give access to Mystery".[131]

107. I ask *everyone* to look more deeply at man, whom Christ has saved in the mystery of

[131] JOHN PAUL II, Address to the University of Krakow for the 600th Anniversary of the Jagiellonian University (8 June 1997), 4: *L'Osservatore Romano*, 9-10 June 1997, 12.

his love, and at the human being's unceasing search for truth and meaning. Different philosophical systems have lured people into believing that they are their own absolute master, able to decide their own destiny and future in complete autonomy, trusting only in themselves and their own powers. But this can never be the grandeur of the human being, who can find fulfilment only in choosing to enter the truth, to make a home under the shade of Wisdom and dwell there. Only within this horizon of truth will people understand their freedom in its fullness and their call to know and love God as the supreme realization of their true self.

108.   I turn in the end to the woman whom the prayer of the Church invokes as *Seat of Wisdom*, and whose life itself is a true parable illuminating the reflection contained in these pages. For between the vocation of the Blessed Virgin and the vocation of true philosophy there is a deep harmony. Just as the Virgin was called to offer herself entirely as human being and as woman that God's Word might take flesh and come among us, so too philosophy is called to offer its rational and critical resources that theology, as the understanding of faith, may be fruitful and creative. And just as in giving her assent to Gabriel's word, Mary lost nothing of her true humanity and freedom, so too when philosophy heeds the summons of the Gospel's truth its autonomy is in no way impaired. Indeed, it is then

that philosophy sees all its enquiries rise to their highest expression. This was a truth which the holy monks of Christian antiquity understood well when they called Mary "the table at which faith sits in thought".[132] In her they saw a lucid image of true philosophy and they were convinced of the need to *philosophari in Maria*.

May Mary, Seat of Wisdom, be a sure haven for all who devote their lives to the search for wisdom. May their journey into wisdom, sure and final goal of all true knowing, be freed of every hindrance by the intercession of the one who, in giving birth to the Truth and treasuring it in her heart, has shared it forever with all the world.

Given in Rome, at Saint Peter's, on 14 September, the Feast of the Triumph of the Cross, in the year 1998, the twentieth of my Pontificate.

Joannes Paulus PP. II

---

[132] "*Hē noēra tēs pisteōs trapeza*": Pseudo-Epiphanius, *Homily in Praise of Holy Mary Mother of God*: PG 43, 493.

INDEX

CHAPTER V

THE INTERVENTIONS OF THE MAGISTERIUM
IN PHILOSOPHICAL MATTERS

CHAPTER VI

THE INTERACTION
BETWEEN THEOLOGY AND PHILOSOPHY

CHAPTER VII

CURRENT REQUIREMENTS
AND TASKS

MAGISTERIUM — Series